MARCUS GARVEY, HERO

MARCUS GARVEY, HERO

A First Biography

Tony Martin

The New Marcus Garvey Library, No. 3

Black Classic Press
Baltimore

Marcus Garvey, Hero: A First Biography

Copyright 1983 by Tony Martin
Published 2022 by Black Classic Press

All Rights Reserved.
Library of Congress Control Number: 2022932478

Print book ISBN: 978-1-57478-189-2
E-book ISBN: 978-1-57478-190-8

Printed by BCP Digital Printing (www.bcpdigital.com)
an affiliate company of Black Classic Press Inc.
For a virtual tour of our publishing and printing facility visit:
https://www.c-span.org/video/?441322-2/tour-black-classic-press

Purchase Black Classic Press books from your favorite bookseller
or online at: www.blackclassicbooks.com

For inquiries or to request a list of titles, write:
Black Classic Press
P.O. Box 13414
Baltimore, MD 21203

Tony Martin and the Majority Press

 Tony Martin (1942-2013) was a preeminent authority on Marcus Garvey and the Universal Negro Improvement Association (UNIA). A native of Trinidad, Martin received his M.A. and Ph.D. from Michigan State University. He was tenured at Wellesley College where he taught for most of his career. He introduced a generation of students and others to Marcus Garvey. Martin's meticulous work solidified Garvey's importance to Pan-African history, the Civil Rights Movement, Black Power and African liberation movements around the world. Martin was one of the earliest scholars to view Garvey's legacy as a lasting testimony in the struggles of Black diasporic people. In 1983, Martin founded The Majority Press. He went on to author and publish other books on Garvey, Pan African culture, and several titles by other authors on related themes.

Black Classic Press is pleased to continue the legacy of Tony Martin by publishing selected titles authored by him and previously published by The Majority Press.

THE NEW MARCUS GARVEY LIBRARY

A Series of Original Works by Tony Martin

No. 1   Literary Garveyism: Garvey, Black Arts and the Harlem Renaissance

No. 2   The Poetical Works of Marcus Garvey

No. 3   Marcus Garvey, Hero: A First Biography

No. 4   Amy Ashwood Garvey: Pan-Africanist, Feminist and Wife No. 1

No. 5   African Fundamentalism: A Literary Anthology of the Garvey Movement

No. 6   The Pan-African Connection: From Slavery to Garvey and Beyond

No. 7   Message to the People: The Course of African Philosophy (By Marcus Garvey, ED by Tony Martin)

No. 8   Race First: The Ideological and Organizational Struggles of Marcus Garvey and the Universal Negro Improvement Association

No. 9   The Philosophy and Opinions of Marcus Garvey (Ed. by Amy Jacques Garvey, Preface by Tony Martin)

To WEA —
Cynthia Fortson, '85, Rita Gordon, '85, Shirdell Lee, '85
and
Judy LaVacca, '84, Nicole Lise, '86 and Ana Rosa, '86
of Wellesley College
and to all my students, past and present.

Courtesy Kwabena O. Prempeh

East Brooklyn, New York,
Garveyites, 1931

Contents

Preface   ix
1   Early Life: 1887–1910   1
2   Travels in Latin America and Europe:
    1910–1914   15
3   Birth of the UNIA: 1914–1916   25
4   From Jamaica to the U.S.A.: 1916–1918   38
5   Garveyism Sweeps the World: 1918–1922   48
6   Garveyism in the West Indies and
    Latin America – 1920s   69
7   Garveyism in Africa – 1920s   85
8   Garveyism in North America, Europe
    and Australia – 1920s   96
9   Enemies Within and Without   100
10   Back to Jamaica: 1927–1935   115
11   Last London Years: 1935–1940   141
12   Marcus Garvey, Hero   148
13   Conclusion   161
    Some Suggestions for Further Reading   165
    Index   167

Marcus Garvey (seated in dark suit with fan) and the Port-of-Spain,
Trinidad City Council, 1937. Mayor Alfred Richards is to Garvey's right.

Preface

This book is designed to fill a long-felt need. It provides a brief, straightforward biography of Marcus Garvey, suitable for use in secondary schools and freshman/sophomore level university courses. At the same time, it incorporates the very latest research into Garvey's life and career, and will therefore be of use to adult readers desiring a quick and accurate introduction to Garvey's life and work.

May 1983   Tony Martin
                            Wellesley, Massachusetts

Garvey, Marley, Selassie I, Jah Rastafari — Independence Square, Port-of-Spain, Trinidad, April 1981.

Photo: Tony Martin

1

Early Life: 1887-1910

The West Indies in the Late Nineteenth Century

The West Indies in 1887, the year of Marcus Garvey's birth in Jamaica, was not an easy place for the Afro West Indians who formed the majority of the population in most territories. Slavery had finally ended in 1838 in nearly all of the British islands and as recently as 1886 in Cuba. Many of the Afro-West Indians alive during young Garvey's childhood would therefore have been slaves at some point in their lives.

The end of slavery had meant some relief from the harsher aspects of life under that system, but it did not mean automatic equality with the slavemasters and their children. The bulk of the Afro-West Indian population in 1887 was poor. Many eked out an existence as peasant farmers on small plots of land. Often such plots were owned by large landowners and peasants had to hand over a portion of their harvest as rent. Many of the ex-slaves and their children and grandchildren still laboured on the sugarcane and other plantations, as in the days of slavery. Their wages were low and working conditions hard. A million new immigrants were brought into the West Indies to ensure that the slaveowning class would continue to have a large supply of cheap labour. Most of these immigrants came from India, but others came from China, Portugal, Java, Africa, Afro-America, Indo-China, Japan and Northern Europe.

Nor did the ex-slaves have any political power worth mentioning. Political power was firmly in the hands of the British, French, Dutch and other European governments which ruled the islands. Here and there in the British islands small numbers of elected members were allowed onto the various legislative bodies, but the time was still many years off, when non-white West Indians would serve in appreciable numbers on such councils. Most Afro-West Indians in the late nineteenth century, and indeed as late as the 1950s in some islands, could not vote. Voting was restricted to persons owning sizeable amounts of property or earning large incomes. Well over ninety percent of the population was thereby denied the privilege of voting.

The depressed condition of the Afro-West Indian population extended into the field of education. Primary schools had been started for the ex-slaves but as the nineteenth century neared its end, illiteracy was still widespread. A popular history of Jamaica reports that only 22,000 of that island's quarter of a million Blacks could write in 1883. Some of the well-known prestige secondary schools, such as St. Mary's College and Queen's Royal College in Trinidad, had already been founded, but they still catered mainly to white students. In the area of higher education the situation was even more hopeless. Codrington College in Barbados served a small number of students, mainly in theology. There were a few other insignificant and short-lived efforts at university education, but for all practical purposes there was no university education in the British Caribbean. Those aspiring to higher education had to leave home. These would include the exceptionally brilliant (the one or two from each territory who won a government scholarship each year); the very rich, who could afford to spend three or more years at Oxford, Cambridge, London, Edinburgh or elsewhere in the British Isles; and the poor but highly ambitious, who usually tried to work their way through school in North America, especially in Afro-American colleges and universities. In an earlier period Europeans had seriously debated whether Africans were capable of being educated at all, and in the early 18th century, Francis Williams, an Afro-Jamaican, was actually sent to Cambridge University as an experiment. He graduated successfully, wrote Latin poetry and was unable to fit comfortably back into Jamaican society. But his success, such as it was, did not move the British authorities to provide university education for the Black masses.

Still, there were four professions for which it was possible to study without leaving the West Indies. These were teaching, law (for solicitors only—barristers had to qualify in England), pharmacy and the ministry (for Protestant denominations). Many enterprising Blacks and coloureds seized the opportunity these professions provided to rise out of poverty.

The West Indies of the late nineteenth century was also a place dominated by strange notions of race and colour. The white former slaveowners and their descendants, together with European administrators, occupied the highest rungs in the social ladder. The African ex-slaves and their descendants were mostly on the bottom. In between were the coloureds or people of mixed race. Marcus Garvey once traced the origin of the coloured class to the "old slave owners" who "raped their female slaves, married or unmarried, and compelled them into polygamy much against their will, thus producing the 'coloured' element."

Although there was always a handful of Blacks who, through exceptional ability, very hard work, luck, or all three, could rise above the condition of their fellows, they were nothing but a small minority. Between the three major racial groups were rigid walls of prejudice. Whites often lived in exclusive neighbourhoods which were segregated in all but name. Whites did not allow coloureds and Blacks into their social clubs or football and cricket teams. Coloureds did not allow Blacks into theirs. In the police force and army, Afro-West Indians could rise as high as sergeant and no higher. All the commissioned officers were white. In the Civil Service the higher posts were normally reserved for whites. Marcus Garvey in 1913 described what happened in Jamaica when, for a brief moment, the Civil Service had been thrown open to competitive exams. He wrote,

... when the Government twenty or thirty years ago threw open the doors of the Civil Service to competitive examination, the Negro youths swept the board and captured every available office, leaving their white competitors far behind. This system went on for a few years, but as the white youths were found to be intellectually inferior to the black, the whites persuaded the Government to abolish the competitive system and fill vacancies by nomination, and by this means kept out the black youths. The service has long since been recruited from an inferior class of sycophantic weaklings whose brains are exhausted by dissipation and vice before they reach the age of thirty-five.

Even in department stores and other commercial establishments, Afro-West Indians often would not be employed, except as cleaners, labourers and suchlike.

Because of the barriers against advancement at home, Afro-West Indians in the late nineteenth century were emigrating in their tens of thousands in search of new opportunities for employment, education and political and social improvement. Many from the Windward and Leeward Islands moved to Trinidad and Guyana (then British Guiana). Many more moved further afield.

Panama at this time was the most popular destination for West Indian emigrants. From as early as the 1860s, West Indians were attracted there to work on railway construction. From 1879 to 1888 the French tried to build a Panama Canal and thousands more

flocked there. When in 1904 the United States resumed work on the Canal, thousands more went over.

By the 1880s West Indians were also going in sizeable numbers to Costa Rica (to build railways and
later to work on banana plantations), Mexico and the
United States. By the early twentieth century they
had spread all over Central America, and northern
South America, to such places as Nicaragua, Honduras, Guatemala, Colombia, Ecuador and Venezuela.
These emigrants made more money overseas than
they had done at home. They were legendary for
the devotion with which they saved their earnings
and sent sizeable quantities back to the families they
had left behind. Yet, life was no paradise in these new
found lands. West Indian workers were often ill-
treated. In the 1880s Jamaicans were attacked by
Colombian troops at Culebra in Panama. And from
1904 on the Panama Canal, West Indians had to live
with the kind of extreme racism for which the southern United States was well-known. White workers on
the Canal were known as "gold" employees, while
the Blacks were classified as "silver" employees. The
silver employees received inferior working conditions
and less pay and were subjected to all kinds of racist
practices, including segregation. In addition, many
emigrants died of disease in the malaria-infested
swamps through which the Canal was constructed.

Jamaicans and Barbadians usually predominated
among the emigrants, but all of the British West Indies
were represented. While many emigrants worked for
a while, saved some money and came back home,
many others stayed abroad. From Jamaica alone, if

one subtracts the number of returning workers from
those who stayed abroad, one is left with a net emigration of 69,000 persons for the years 1881 to 1911.
Of these, 43,000 went to Panama, 16,000 to the
United States and 10,000 to other places. Many of
those who went to Central and South America later
moved on to Cuba, the United States or elsewhere,
especially after the Panama Canal was completed in
1914. Many, however, stayed on in their adopted
homes and their descendants now form the bulk of
the Black populations in places such as Panama and
Costa Rica.

A fair number of Afro-West Indians of the late
nineteenth century had actually been born in Africa.
Many more would have had parents and grandparents
born there. And with the freedom that came with
emancipation had come also a freedom to express
their deep interest in the African Motherland. Mandingoes from Trinidad asked to be sent back home to
West Africa and at least one succeeded in making it
back to the Gambia. In the 1850s, churchmen from
Codrington College in Barbados established a mission
in the Rio Pongo area of what is now Guinea. In that
same decade Edward Wilmot Blyden emigrated from
St. Thomas in the Virgin Islands to Liberia, via the
United States. In time he became one of the greatest
of nineteenth century African scholars and statesmen
and was a favourite author of the young Marcus
Garvey. In 1865 three hundred and forty-six Barba-
badians emigrated to Liberia, partly due to the influence of Blyden. One of them, Arthur Barclay, eventually became president of Liberia, from 1904 to

1912. His son, Edwin, served as secretary of state and acting president. Around 1900 several thousand Cubans were trying to return to their homes in the Belgian Congo (now Zaire). Some succeeded. Many more West Indians not only returned to Africa, but did what little they could to speak out on Africa's behalf, especially during the conquest of most of Africa by Europe, which took place after 1860. Among these was Henry Sylvester Williams, a Trinidad lawyer, who organized a Pan-African Conference in London in 1900. Here West Indians, Africans and Afro-Americans examined the problems facing peoples of African origin all over the world and petitioned Queen Victoria of England to improve the conditions facing Africans in South Africa.

Marcus Garvey—Childhood and Youth

It was into this world of poverty and ambition, emigration and Africa-consciousness, that Marcus Mosiah Garvey was born, on the 17th of August 1887. The place was St. Ann's Bay in the parish of St. Ann on Jamaica's north coast. He was the last of eleven children, all of whom died in childhood except for a sister, Indiana. His parents were Marcus and Sarah Garvey, and the family was reasonably comfortable, compared with the average peasant of that time. Mr. Garvey was a stonemason by trade. He read widely, was consequently well-informed and a respected figure in the community. He was stern and withdrawn and never developed a close relationship with his son. He was said to be a descendant of Jamaica's maroons, the well-known African slaves who escaped to the hills and forced the British to recognize their virtual independence, even during the days of slavery. Mrs. Garvey was quite unlike her husband. Marcus once described her as a "sober and conscientious Christian, too soft and good for the time in which she lived."

Marcus loved St. Ann's Bay. Years later he would write—"I was born in the beautiful Parish of St. Ann, near the falls of the Roaring River. I grew with nature and drank much of her inspiration. . . ." His boyhood days were active and full of varied experiences. He was a strong boy and well-liked by his playmates, who looked up to him as somewhat of a leader. He swam in the sea, played cricket, and ran and cycled with his friends. Two white families, one of them the local Wesleyan minister, owned property adjoining the Garveys, and so Marcus' early playmates included some white children. As he entered his teens, however, he noticed that first the girls and later the boys among his white friends shunned his company and pretended not to know him. These were his first lessons in racial distinctions.

Like most active youngsters, Marcus had his narrow escapes from disaster. On one occasion he escaped from a shark. On another his mother saved him from eating an avocado pear contaminated by rat poison. He and some friends were once hauled before juvenile court for stoning the windows of a church and school. Marcus was fined one pound and his father, wanting to teach him a lesson, refused to pay. His mother paid the fine and saved her son from a spell in reform school.

On the more positive side, Marcus pumped the organ at the local Wesleyan church and helped his mother and her brother on a small plot of land which they farmed as tenants of a landowner. Many years later, in 1929, Marcus recalled that he received 13 shillings a week for selling bananas from this land. With that money, he said, "I used to go to Sunday School and when the girls were looking, threw 4 shillings in the collection plate."

There was nothing extraordinary about Marcus' early education but it was still above average, compared with the widespread illiteracy of the time. He attended primary school and, like so many West Indian students, received private lessons in some secondary school subjects. Marcus was lucky in that he was able to read widely from his father's library. This was an invaluable supplement to his formal education. And, in the absence of a secondary education, he was again lucky to get something which turned out to be a good substitute and a great asset in his later life. Even before he left school, he began learning a trade. He was apprenticed to a printer, who also happened to be his godfather, Mr. Burrows. Mr. Burrows, like Mr. Garvey, was fond of books and kept a library, and young Marcus was again able to read widely and deepen his knowledge of history, world affairs and other subjects.

Marcus Moves to Kingston

Marcus quickly mastered the printing trade. Then, after a few years, he decided to try his hand at the city. His mother had suffered great financial loss in a hurricane of 1903 which had destroyed her crops. Marcus also yearned for wider horizons to explore and, maybe, conquer. At the age of sixteen, therefore, he arrived in Kingston, where he stayed with one of his mother's brothers. He obtained work at P.A. Benjamin's printery and, at the early age of eighteen, was promoted to foreman. This was a big achievement for an Afro-Jamaican of any age at that time, for the normal practice was to import foremen from England or Canada. Marcus at eighteen also had the distinction of being the youngest foreman printer in Kingston.

As soon as he established himself in Kingston, Marcus sent for his mother, in hopes of helping her over the loss of her crops. But she did not like the city, and died in less than two years.

Marcus liked the hustle and bustle of the city. People here were well-informed on the political issues of the day. He himself soon joined a group of friends who discussed local and world affairs by the seaside at Victoria Pier on Saturday nights.

The conditions facing his fellow countrymen now became one of Marcus' major concerns. He involved himself in social and community work and when his co-workers formed a Printers Union, one of the earliest trade unions in the British West Indies, he joined it. The new union soon called a strike. Management promised Marcus favourable treatment if he did not participate, but he preferred to side with his workers, who then elected him strike leader. The union received financial help from printers in the United States but one member ran off with the money and the workers were forced to go back to work. Marcus, as their leader, lost his job but got another with the government printery.

Marcus was now becoming a well-known figure around Kingston. In addition to his involvement in workers' struggles and his social work, he began other kinds of activity that he would continue for the rest of his life. One of these was public speaking. He took elocution lessons from Dr. J. Robert Love (1835–1914), Jamaica's leading Black politician of that period. Dr. Love was born in the Bahamas and had studied and worked in the United States for many years. He had also served as a clergyman in Haiti. Love had helped elect Jamaica's first Black legislative council member and in 1906 himself became the second Afro-Jamaican elected to the council. Although a wealthy man, he fought persistently for the rights of Jamaica's poor. He was also a fervent Pan-Africanist, one who was interested in the welfare of African peoples everywhere and especially in Africa itself. For all of these reasons Marcus admired Dr. Love. Love also published a newspaper, the *Jamaica Advocate*, and Marcus was among its most avid readers.

In addition to his elocution lessons, Marcus visited many churches to study the speaking styles of ministers. Back home and alone in his room he would lecture to imaginary audiences in front of his mirror. In 1910, though living in Kingston, he represented his home parish of St. Ann in an islandwide public speaking contest held at the Collegiate Hall, Kingston. For the first round, contestants had to recite a poem and Marcus finished in first place. For the second round, a prose recitation, he delivered a favourite of his, Lord Chatham's speech to the House of Lords on the United States War of Independence. Someone in the audience heckled him when his voice broke and spoiled his concentration. The result was that he could manage only a disappointing third in the overall standings. Marcus was so upset that he successfully took his heckler to court for maliciously causing him to lose first place. He also began, around this time, to organize public speaking contests among the youth of West Kingston. In later years Marcus would be widely acclaimed as one of the world's greatest orators.

Another lifelong activity that Marcus began in Kingston was journalism. He worked on two newspapers and published a third, his own *Garvey's Watchman,* somewhere around 1910. Garvey's paper was almost certainly named after the *Watchman* of George William Gordon, one of the principal figures in the Jamaica (Morant Bay) Rebellion of 1865. Gordon, a mulatto politician, was hanged on the orders of British Governor Edward John Eyre, who accused him of inciting Black peasants to violent revolt in their quest for land, work and freedom. British troops brought in to put down the uprising butchered about 430 peasants, brutally flogged about 600, including women, and destroyed over 1,000 of the peasants' homes. Garvey felt strongly about the Jamaica Rebellion. In 1913 he wrote

[The ex-slaves] again revolted in 1865 in the East, under the leadership of the Hon. George William Gordon, a member of the Legislative Council, and Paul Bogle. They sounded the call of unmolested liberty, but owing to the suppression of telegraphic communication, they were handicapped and suppressed, otherwise Jamaica would be as free today as Haiti, which threw off the French yoke under the leadership of the famous Negro General, Toussaint L'Ouverture. The Gordon party killed fifteen of the native despots and a savage plutocrat by the name of Baron von Ketelhodt who had great control over the governor, Edward John Eyre. The victorious party hanged Gordon, Paul Bogle and several hundred Negroes, for which crime Governor Eyre was recalled to England and indicted for murder, but escaped by the "skin of his teeth."

In Kingston Marcus also became assistant secretary of a pioneer Jamaican political organization, the National Club. This club was unhappy with the way that British colonialism restricted opportunities for most Jamaicans to advance politically, educationally and economically. It campaigned for more self-government for Jamaicans. Two members of the National Club, S.A.G. Cox and Alexander Dixon, were elected to the legislative council.

By 1910 it was already clear that Marcus Garvey was a young man with a bright future ahead of him. Still only twenty-three years old, he had already made a name for himself as a printer, journalist, orator, social worker and political activist. But he was a restless young man, ever seeking new fields to explore. Jamaicans were by now pouring in their thousands to Central America and other lands in search of a better life. Marcus decided to join the exodus.

2

Travels In Latin America And Europe: 1910-1914

Central and South America

Marcus had a maternal uncle in Costa Rica, and he made this his first stop. His uncle got him a job as a timekeeper on a banana plantation. The United Fruit Company, a giant United States corporation, owned huge banana and sugar-cane plantations all over Latin America and the Caribbean (including Jamaica itself), and many West Indian emigrants to foreign lands ended up working for it.

Marcus kept his job on the plantation for a short time and then worked on the docks at the Caribbean Sea port of Port Limón, where most of the West Indians in Costa Rica settled. But this type of work was not his main concern. For him it was simply a means of raising enough money to get started in his new surroundings. His main concern here was to observe the conditions facing West Indian workers and do what little he could to help better their lot.

Conditions in Costa Rica could be harsh for West Indians. Some were robbed and killed by bandits and sometimes they lost their money in banks that went out of business. There was no organized body to look after their interests. Most were British subjects, but the British diplomatic officials showed little interest in protecting their welfare. Marcus started a newspaper, *La Nación (The Nation)*, as a means of reaching the immigrants and getting them organized. Soon he was as familiar a figure as he had been in Kingston and the Costa Rican and British authorities began to look upon him with suspicion. As far as they were concerned, he was nothing but a troublemaker. Nor did the United Fruit Company take kindly to the idea of Marcus trying to organize their workers. One of their representatives described him as "a typical noisy Jamaican" who "if allowed to go on as he has been doing," might end up being a second Toussaint L'Ouverture. Some say that Marcus was eventually jailed in Costa Rica. Some think that he was deported. One thing is certain—the authorities were not sorry to see him go.

Marcus now systematically travelled through the West Indian immigrant communities of Central and South America. His widow, Amy Jacques Garvey, has written that he visited Guatemala, Nicaragua, Panama (Bocas-del-Toro and Colón), Ecuador, Chile and Peru. In Colón, Panama, he again published a small newspaper, this time called *La Prensa (The Press)*. A Trinidadian, Mr. J. Charles Zampty, originally from Belmont, Port-of-Spain, recalled having met Marcus in Panama about 1912. At the time Marcus was addressing a group of West Indian workers who had formed themselves into the Colón Federal Labour Union.

Marcus' travels in Latin America were an eye opener. Everywhere he found the same story of immigrant workers enduring the most abominable hardships in their efforts to make a living. Unemployment and discrimination at home had forced them to seek a living in strange lands hundreds and thousands of miles away. Like soldiers gone to war, some fell a long way from home, never to see their native lands again. Some did succeed in accumulating money and returning home. But for most, including many of these more fortunate ones, the experience was a hard one.

Marcus returned to Jamaica, in the words of his widow, "sickened with fever, and sick at heart over appeals from his people for help on their behalf." But he did not linger long. His curiosity was aroused and there were other places to check out. His sister, Indiana, had gone off to England as governess for the children of a wealthy Jamaican family, and with her help Marcus soon found himself in London.

England and Europe

West Indian emigration to England at that time was insignificant, compared with the mass exodus to Latin America. Yet, there had been small communities of Black people in England at various periods going back several hundreds of years. The slave trade had deposited quite a few Africans in England and Queen Elizabeth I had passed a law banning them from her kingdom in 1601. In 1772 the English chief justice, Lord Mansfield, had outlawed slavery in England (though not in the British colonies) in a case involving a Jamaican slave, James Somerset, who had been brought to England. Freedom for these slaves turned out to be freedom to starve, because no one would employ them. By 1787 so many were destitute that a group of English humanitarians procured a spot on the West African coast (Sierra Leone) where the "blackpoor," as they were called, could return and live a life free of English discrimination.

When Garvey arrived in England in 1912 there were small communities of Africans, West Indians and sometimes other people of colour in several British cities. Some of these were students and could be found in London, Edinburgh and other university centers. Many were seamen. These lived, usually in extreme poverty, near the docks in such seaport cities as London, Liverpool, Cardiff and Hull. It was difficult for Black seamen to obtain work in Britain. Often African and West Indian seamen would be discharged from one ship in Britain and would have to wait so long to be hired on another that they found themselves gradually settling permanently around the dock areas. In 1919 there were bloody racial riots, some of the most serious in British history, when these seaport Black communities were attacked by white mobs. Most of the other Blacks in England in Garvey's time came as visitors or members of delegations protesting conditions in British colonies.

In Britain Marcus found employment on the docks at London, Liverpool and Cardiff, much as he had done at Port Limón. He met African seamen who told him about life in their home countries.

Ever ambitious, he attended lectures in law at Birkbeck College in London. Speakers' Corner at London's Hyde Park fascinated him. Here, every weekend, people of all description set up their make-shift soapboxes and addressed the curious crowds who gathered to hear them. Marcus could not resist this temptation and soon joined the soapbox orators. He was also a frequent visitor to the public galleries of the House of Commons. Here he observed, with great interest, the debates in the parliament which controlled the destiny of the British West Indies and the rest of the far-flung empire on which, as the British were fond of boasting, the sun never set.

Marcus also continued his journalistic activity. He did not publish a newspaper in England, but he wrote articles which appeared in various publications. In between this hectic round of activity he travelled widely through the British Isles and also visited France, Italy, Spain, Austria, Hungary and Germany.

This pace proved too much for Marcus' slender resources and by July 1913 he found himself back in London and penniless. His sister had returned to Jamaica after five years in England and there was no other close friend or relative that he could turn to. He therefore sought help from the Colonial Office, the agency of the British government which administered the colonies. Before they could decide on his request, however, he received one of the biggest breaks of his English trip. This was a job at the *Africa Times and Orient Review.*

The *Africa Times and Orient Review* was an excellent magazine which described itself as both Pan-African (that is, concerned with the welfare of peoples

of African origin the world over) and Pan-Oriental
(concerned with the struggles of all Eastern peoples).
Its scope therefore included most of what is nowa-
days often called the Third World. Most of the world's
important nationalist struggles against European
colonialism were covered in the magazine. Among the
authors or subjects of articles were such eminent persons as Booker T. Washington, the Afro-American
educator and Edward Wilmot Blyden, the West Indian
born West African statesman and scholar. Reading the
issues of this magazine was, for Marcus, a veritable
course in Black and Third World Studies. In addition,
the magazine's offices served as a meeting place for
African, Afro-American, West Indian and Asian visitors to London, many of them important personalities
in their home countries.

The editor of the *Africa Times and Orient Review*
was Dusé Mohamed Ali, an African. One of his parents
was from the Sudan and the other from Egypt. He
had travelled widely as an actor and had settled in
London. He later became an official of Marcus' organization in the United States. Still later he became a
newspaper publisher in Nigeria.

An article written by Marcus appeared in the
October 1913 issue of the *Africa Times and Orient
Review*. It was entitled "The British West Indies in
the Mirror of Civilization" and is the earliest of his
published articles available to historians at the present
time. The article gave evidence of a fine writing style
and a good grasp of West Indian history. It began, "In
these days when democracy is spreading itself over
the British Empire, and the peoples under the rule of

the Union Jack are freeing themselves from hereditary lordship, and an unjust bureaucracy, it should not be amiss to recount the condition of affairs in the British West Indies, and particularly, in the historic island of Jamaica, one of the oldest colonial possessions of the Crown." William H. Ferris, an Afro-American scholar and graduate of Harvard and Yale universities, was sufficiently impressed by this article to write the magazine congratulating Garvey.

Marcus concluded the article by making two interesting prophesies. The first involved West Indian federation. He said, "There have been several movements to federate the British West Indian Islands, but owing to parochial feelings nothing definite has been achieved. Ere long this change is sure to come about because the people of these islands are all one. They live under the same conditions, are of the same race and mind, and have the same feelings and sentiments regarding the things of the world."

The second prediction concerned the glorious future which awaited the African race, and the role which West Indians would play in bringing it about. "As one who knows the people well," he declared, "I make no apology for prophesying that there will soon be a turning point in the history of the West Indies; and that the people who inhabit that portion of the Western Hemisphere will be the instruments of uniting a scattered race who, before the close of many centuries, will found an Empire on which the sun shall shine as ceaselessly as it shines on the empire of the North today." This might seem like a joke, Garvey added, but would not the Roman general,

Julius Caesar, have laughed in 55 B.C. if someone had told him that the primitive English he was about to conquer would someday rule the largest empire in history? So, he concluded, "Laugh then you may, at what I have been bold enough to prophesy, but as surely as there is an evolution in the natural growth of man and nations, so surely will there be a change in the history of these subjected regions."

Marcus ran into financial problems again in May 1914. This time a human rights organization, the Anti-slavery and Aborigines Protection Society, began discussions with the Colonial Office on paying his passage back to Jamaica. Marcus managed to raise the money on his own and left England on June 17, 1914.

Courtesy Dr. Anyim Palmer

**Architect's Drawing of Marcus Garvey School,
Los Angeles, California — 1983**

UNIA Women, 1921

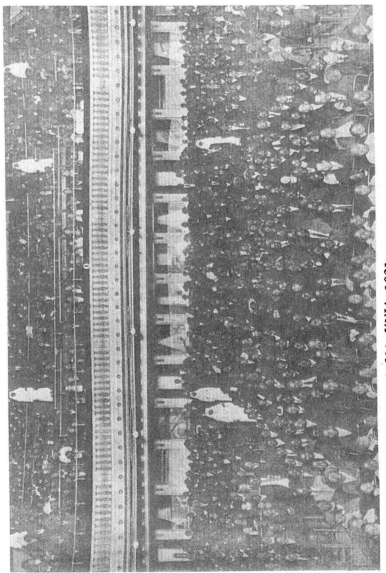

Sunday meeting of the Cincinnati, Ohio UNIA, 1921.

3

Birth Of The UNIA: 1914-1916

The Call to Leadership

As he left the port of Southampton on that June day in 1914, Marcus Garvey could look back on four years of intensive further preparation for the life's work that lay ahead. Through Central and South America, through Great Britain and Europe, he had travelled. He had lived in Black communities, worked amongst the people, shared their joys and sorrows. He had agitated on their behalf and noted their weakness. And he had listened, learnt and reflected on what he had seen.

In London, on his return from Europe, Marcus had also read Booker T. Washington's autobiography, *Up From Slavery*. Born a slave in the United States, Washington had worked his way to become founder of Tuskegee Institute in Alabama, the most famous Black-controlled educational establishment in the world. In the field of politics, he had become the most powerful Black man in the United States. In big ways and small, he had been able to help large numbers of his people.

Up From Slavery had a tremendous impact on Marcus. He then and there realized his "doom," as he put it, of becoming a leader of his people. Writing some years later, he recalled—"I asked: 'Where is the Black man's government?' 'Where is his King and his Kingdom?' 'Where is his president, his country, and his ambassador, his army, his navy, his men of big affairs?' I could not find them and then I declared, 'I will help to make them.'" The slow boat trip back to Jamaica took almost a month and Marcus had enough time to think further about his decision. "Becoming naturally restless for the opportunity of doing something for the advancement of my race," he said of his last days in London, "I was determined that the black man would not continue to be kicked about by all the other races and nations of the world, as I saw it in the West Indies, South and Central America and Europe, and as I read of it in America." Marcus' enthusiasm for his future work now could not be contained. "My young and ambitious mind," he wrote, "led me into flights of great imagination. I saw before me then, even as I do now, a new world of black men, not peons, serfs, dogs and slaves, but a nation of sturdy men making their impress upon civilization and causing a new light to dawn upon the human race."

One of Marcus' fellow travellers on the trip home was a West Indian man who had lived in Basutoland (now called Lesotho), a British colony totally surrounded by South Africa. He brought with him a Basuto wife. Marcus already had some knowledge of conditions in European-ruled Africa, but what this man told him was worse than anything he had heard yet. "He related to me such horrible and pitiable tales," Marcus remembered, "that my heart bled within me."

Yet, the trip home was not totally devoted to serious reflection and discussion. The ship stopped at Port-of-Spain, Trinidad on its way to Jamaica and Marcus received an opportunity to do some sightseeing. This was his first visit to the island and he had no close friends there. As he strolled through the streets of Port-of-Spain, just another face in the crowd, he could not have guessed that in a mere five years time, his would be one of the most revered names on the island. How could he have imagined that by 1919 the leaders of the most powerful workers' organization, the Trinidad Workingmen's Association, would be members of his soon-to-be-founded Universal Negro Improvement Association? Or that his newspaper, the *Negro World*, would be banned by the Trinidad government? Or that some of his followers who happened to be born in Grenada and Jamaica would be deported from the island? Yet, these things were soon to be.

Universal Negro Improvement Association

Marcus arrived in Kingston, Jamaica, on July 15, 1914. Five days later he founded the Universal Negro Improvement and Conservation Association and African Communities (Imperial) League. "Conservation"

and "Imperial" were later dropped from the title.
Most people over the years have known it simply as
the Universal Negro Improvement Association, or
UNIA. The title of the new organization revealed
Marcus' desire to improve the condition of Africans
all over the world, be they in the West Indies, Afro-
America, Africa itself or anywhere else. Marcus used
the word "Negro" as a convenient means of denoting
all persons of African descent. Since the 1960s, however, the word has become unpopular, due to its
slavery origins. "African," "Afro-American" and
"Black" are among the terms now widely used in
place of "Negro."

Conditions in the West Indies have already been
described. Conditions in Africa and Afro-America
were as bad, if not worse. Despite four hundred years
of the transatlantic slave trade, most of Africa had
remained independent of European domination up
until the early nineteenth century. But in the half
century or so before 1914, practically the whole continent had been conquered by European nations, in
what history books call the "Scramble for Africa." So
great was this scramble that European nations seemed
on the verge of going to war among themselves as
each one tried to gobble up as much of the continent
as it could. The threat of war was lessened by the
Berlin Conference of 1884-1885, where the Europeans decided instead of fighting to sit around the
conference table and discuss who should get what
parts of Africa. Only Ethiopia and Liberia escaped
European colonialism. Ethiopia, under the Emperor
Menelik II, crushed an invading Italian army at the

Battle of Aduwa in 1896. Liberia, established as a home for Afro-American ex-slaves, had been independent since 1847.

Even after the end of slavery in the Western Hemisphere, forced labour (practically slavery under a different name) continued in some parts of Africa. And the conquest of Africa had been followed by the slaughter of millions of Africans, on a scale far greater than anything happening in the West Indies or Afro-America at that time. In the Belgian Congo alone, an estimated 8 to 20 million Africans were killed in twenty years or so near the end of the nineteenth century. As in the West Indies, Africans in 1914 had almost no political power. Illiteracy was widespread.

The same tale of woe could be told about Afro-America. Here slavery had ended in 1865. In that year, about 95 per cent of Afro-Americans were illiterate. Soon after slavery ended, Afro-Americans were given the right to vote and to be elected to legislative bodies. But by 1914, most of them had lost these rights as state after state passed laws preventing Black people from voting. In the South, where the vast majority of Black people lived, segregation laws forced Blacks to live in inferior areas, go to inferior schools, travel in the back of the bus and receive less pay for equal labour. In addition, lynching, a practice unknown in the West Indies in 1914, was rampant. Lynching consisted of the public murder of Afro-Americans by mobs of white people, usually for no justifiable reason. Thousands of Black people of all ages and both sexes were hanged, shot, burned at the stake and/or beaten to death at street corners, in parks and in other public places. Sometimes lynchings were even advertised in advance, to encourage large crowds of spectators. The murderers were not normally apprehended, though they performed their acts in the open.

By 1914, thousands of Afro-Americans were leaving their traditional homes in the South, in hopes of escaping these harsh conditions. They were moving to large northern cities, such as New York, Chicago, Detroit and Philadelphia.

Haiti was the only independent predominantly African country outside of Africa in 1914. But it was soon to lose its independence, for United States military forces invaded it in 1915. The North Americans remained until 1934. It was for all these reasons then, that Marcus Garvey, as he looked around the world of 1914, had to ask himself, "Where is the black man's government?"

Marcus was elected president and travelling commissioner of the Universal Negro Improvement Association. Among the fifteen members of the "board of management" were his sister, Indiana, her husband, Alfred Peart and Amy Ashwood. Amy was only seventeen years old and had attended Westwood Training College for Women. She was beautiful, intelligent and talented. Marcus, shortly after his arrival home, had attended a debate at the East Queen Street Baptist Church Hall. There he listened as Amy Ashwood defended the proposition that "Morality does not increase with the march of civilization." He was impressed and struck up a friendship. Amy Ashwood became one of the first members of the UNIA and general secretary of the Ladies' Division. Five years later she became Marcus' first wife.

The early officers and members of the UNIA were similar to Marcus in many ways. They were ambitious people who had worked hard, sometimes in spite of humble beginnings, to improve themselves. They were politically aware and artistically inclined. Some had been active in small political organizations, trade unions, literary and debating societies, informal discussion groups and sporting clubs. Some had known Marcus before his departure from Jamaica. They looked forward to the day when Jamaica would be self-governing and free from racial prejudice. They felt a great bond of kinship with other peoples of African descent around the world and sympathized with other struggling peoples everywhere. Some, like J. Coleman Beecher and A. Bain Alves, would be known as political activists or labour leaders for several years to come.

One of the first tasks of the UNIA was to publish a list of aims and objectives. These included "general" objects relating to African peoples all over the world and "local" objects pertaining to Jamaica. They were as follows—

GENERAL OBJECTS

To establish a Universal Confraternity among the race.

To promote the spirit of race pride and love.

To reclaim the fallen of the race.

To administer to and assist the needy.

To assist in civilizing the backward tribes of Africa.

To strengthen the Imperialism of independent African States.

To establish Commissionaries or Agencies in the principal countries of the world for the protection of all Negroes, irrespective of nationality.

To promote a conscientious spiritual worship among the native tribes of Africa.

To establish Universities, Colleges and Secondary Schools for the further education and culture of the boys and girls of the race.

To conduct a worldwide commercial and industrial intercourse.

LOCAL (JAMAICAN) OBJECTS

To establish educational and industrial (day and evening) colleges for the further education and culture of our boys and girls.

To reclaim the fallen and degraded (especially the criminal class) and help them to a state of good citizenship.

To work among, administer to and assist the needy.

To promote a better taste for commerce and industry.

To rescue the fallen women of the island from the pit of infamy and vice.

To promote a cordial relationship between all men and strengthen the bonds of brotherhood.

To do all that is possible and reasonable to help the struggling masses to a higher state of moral appreciation.

To help generally in the development of the country.

The new organization also adopted a motto which was soon to become very famous—One God! One Aim! One Destiny! It rented offices at 30 Charles Street in downtown Kingston.

In the beginning, the UNIA did not seem very different from most other West Indian charitable organizations, then and now. It entertained and fed hundreds of poor and sick people, especially on Emancipation Day (August 1st) and at Christmas. It opened an employment bureau to help those out of work and planned to set up an industrial farm and institute. The idea here was to lessen unemployment by giving poor people marketable skills. It hoped to run a night school for adults in connection with the farm and institute. And the UNIA ladies sold artificial flowers to raise funds for this charitable work.

Literary and debating societies were popular in those days and the UNIA served as such a society also. Weekly meetings usually included a debate on some interesting subject. This was an excellent means of informing the membership on historical matters and current affairs. The feminist movement of the time was also reflected in such debate topics as "Is the intellect of woman as highly developed as that of man's?" (Marcus argued for the affirmative), and "Women or men, whose influence is more felt in the world?"

Debates were not the only literary activity. The young UNIA held several fundraising concerts. Here, persons would recite from the works of poets such as Longfellow and the Afro-American, Paul Laurence Dunbar. Skits were also performed. Lectures, too, were regularly presented. Sometimes Garvey himself

would speak. Sometimes others, including guest lec-
turers from outside the UNIA, would address the
meeting. And Marcus naturally used the organization
to further his love for elocution contests. He himself
once won the first prize of a gold-filled watch for his
rendition of "Chatham on the American War." To
round it all off, the UNIA ran a library and reading
room.

Marcus insisted from the beginning that the UNIA
was not a political party. This did not mean that it
was not interested in the political events of the day.
For example, like most West Indians of all races at the
beginning of the First World War (1914-1918), Marcus
and the UNIA supported the British king and government against the Germans. (This support turned to
widespread resentment later on, due to the mistreat-
ment of Black West Indian soldiers). In the political
field the young UNIA in January 1915 also protested
a bill in the United States Senate, which sought to
block West Indian immigration to the U.S.A. Marcus
said that such a law would make it even more difficult than it already was, for West Indian students to
obtain a university education.

At first some influential white persons such as the
governor and a Scottish clergyman helped the UNIA.
They could find nothing wrong with just another
harmless charitable organization, or so the UNIA
seemed. Later, they would change their minds, but
not yet. In October 1914 the governor, Sir William
H. Manning, even donated some money to the association.

The most severe opposition at the beginning came
from the coloured group and some of the better-off

Blacks. "I never really knew there was so much colour prejudice in Jamaica, my own native home," Marcus confessed later, "until I started the work of the Universal Negro Improvement Association." He continued, "nobody wanted to be a Negro. . . . Men and women as black as I, and even more so, had believed themselves white under the West Indian order of society. I was simply an impossible man to use openly the term 'Negro;' yet every one beneath his breath was calling the black man a nigger." Marcus was now faced, as he saw it, with an alternative—"I had to decide whether to please my friends and be one of the 'black-whites' of Jamaica, and be reasonably prosperous, or come out openly, and defend and help improve and protect the integrity of the black millions, and suffer. I decided to do the latter. . . ."

Though Marcus' main intention was to lift up his people, he never had any hesitation in frankly pointing out their weaknesses. Some people thought his criticisms too harsh. Yet, a careful reading of his remarks will show that behind his harsh words was a burning desire to rescue his people from ignorance and poverty. In August 1915, Marcus delivered such a critical speech at the Collegiate Hall in Kingston. For days afterwards the newspapers carried letters attacking what he had said. Typical of his remarks that night was the following passage—"Kingston and its environs are so infested with the uncouth and vulgar of our people that we of the cultured class feel positively ashamed to move about, and through this state of affairs some of our most representative men even flatter themselves to believe that they are not of us and practically refuse to identify themselves with the people. Well, this society [UNIA] has set itself the task to go up among the people and help them up. . . ." He declared that Black people should not look to whites for charity forever. "What we lack," he advised, "is self-help, and self-reliance. . . . We are always wanting somebody to do something for us. . . . My opinion is that we are too envious, malicious and superficial, and because of this we keep back ourselves and eventually keep back the country."

These were strong words and seemingly very negative and disparaging. But there was one saving feature. They were not criticism simply for the sake of criticism. They were intended to be followed by positive action to right the wrongs he complained about. Some of his attackers did not see it this way. One of them wrote, "his disgraceful utterances [are] nothing but a rank insult to the Negro race. . . ."

Yet Marcus moved on, for he was determined. He said in the same controversial speech, "those who desire to serve the people must be prepared for the criticism of the unjust and uncharitable." In 1916 he wrote, in a private letter, that he believed himself "called to service in the interest of his unfortunate people."

Sometime in 1914, Marcus began to correspond with Booker T. Washington. He wanted to undertake a lecture tour of the United States to raise funds for the UNIA's industrial farm and institute. He hoped that Washington would help him, especially since the UNIA project would be copied from Washington's own Tuskegee Institute. Washington promised to help but died in November 1915, before Marcus left

Jamaica. Marcus held memorial meetings for him and praised him as an outstanding leader.

Meanwhile, word of the UNIA began to spread overseas. In January 1915 a lady from Antigua wrote Marcus. She had read of the UNIA in the *Christian Science Monitor,* a newspaper published in Boston in the U.S.A. She hoped that the UNIA would extend its work to the other West Indian islands. Later that year the organization itself began to advertise for letters from persons in Colón and Bocas del Toro in Panama, and from Honduras, Guatemala, Nicaragua "and other parts."

Early in 1916 Marcus finally left on his lecture tour of the United States. He expected to be away about five months, but it was to be eleven years and many months before he would return to Jamaica to stay. By then, he would be just about the best known Black man in the whole world.

4

From Jamaica To The U.S.A.: 1916-1918

Harlem

Marcus Garvey arrived in New York on March 23, 1916. By this time the United States had replaced Panama as the major destination for West Indian emigrants. Some 30,000 persons from Jamaica alone moved permanently to the United States between 1911 and 1921. Most of these went to New York. Most West Indians in New York in those days lived in Harlem, the city's major Black community. By 1920 almost one out of every five Black people in Harlem was a West Indian. Many of today's Black native New Yorkers are in fact the descendants of this generation of West Indian emigrants.

Harlem was an immigrant community in other ways too. Most of its population consisted of refugees from the racism of the American South. Even its native New York-born population had only moved there recently from other parts of the city.

Yet, by 1916 this young community was already well on the way to becoming one of the best known in the African world. It was a vibrant, cosmopolitan place, bubbling over with political, cultural and religious activity. There were also overcrowding, rundown neighbourhoods, poverty, police brutality and unemployment. But still the vigour and vitality of the people managed to shine through it all.

Marcus moved in with a Jamaican family in Harlem and got a job as a printer. He also came down with pneumonia. As usual, he did not remain in his job for very long. His mind was on other things. As soon as he saved a few dollars he was off on his lecture tour. He was billed as head of the UNIA of Jamaica and he usually spoke on conditions in his home island or in the Caribbean in general. He let his audiences know that any funds he raised would be going towards the UNIA's industrial farm and institute in Jamaica.

Marcus kicked off his lecture tour with a meeting on May 9, 1916, at St. Mark's Roman Catholic Church Hall at 57 West 138th Street in Harlem. His subject was "Jamaica" and his audience was composed largely of Jamaicans and other West Indians.

He might have hoped for a better beginning, for he is said to have fallen off the platform during the speech.

Thirty-Eight States in a Year

By June he was lecturing in Boston, the second most important center for West Indian-Americans after New York. Over the next year he travelled through thirty-eight of the country's forty-eight states.

A handbill advertising his lecture at the Big Bethel African Methodist Episcopal (AME) Church in Atlanta, Georgia, on March 25, 1917, invited one and all to hear "the Great West Indian Negro Leader, Hon. Marcus Garvey, President of the Universal Negro Improvement Association of Jamaica, West Indies." Marcus' topic was to be " 'The Negroes of the West Indies, after 78 years of Emancipation.' With a general talk on the world position of the race." Whether Marcus himself or the Rev. R. H. Singleton, Big Bethel's pastor, prepared the handbill is not known. But it was a powerful invitation, with clear shades of North American ballyhoo. Few who read it must have been able to resist coming out to hear Marcus speak. "An orator of exceptional force," it proclaimed, though truthfully enough, "Professor Garvey has spoken to packed audiences in England, New York, Boston, Washington, Philadelphia, Chicago, Milwaukee, St. Louis, Detroit, Cleveland, Cincinnati, Indianapolis, Louisville, Nashville, and other cities. He has travelled to the principal countries of Europe, and was the first Negro to speak to the Veterans' Club of London, England." For the difficult to convince who had read this far and had not yet decided to come out and hear the Jamaican orator, there was a parting blast, designed to sweep them right into the audience—"This is the only chance to hear a great man who has taken his message before the world. COME OUT EARLY TO SECURE SEATS. It is worth travelling 1,000 miles to hear."

Apart from lecturing on the West Indies in order to raise funds, Marcus had another interest on his tour through the states—he wanted to observe how Afro-Americans lived and generally study local conditions. He met with some of Afro-America's leading national and local personalities. These included Ida Wells Barnett of Chicago, a leader of the fight against lynching and a prominent figure in Afro-American women's organizations. He also met John Edward Bruce of Yonkers, New York, a well-known journalist and Emmett J. Scott, secretary of Tuskegee Institute in Alabama. Some of his contacts were people he had corresponded with. These in turn would often put him in touch with persons in other cities.

Marcus was very impressed with Afro-America. As he himself put it around November 1917 in Chicago, "I have seen Negro banks in Washington and Chicago, stores, cafes, restaurants, theaters and real estate agencies that fill my heart with joy to realise . . . that at one center of Negrodom, at least, the people of the race have sufficient pride to do things for themselves." Much of the credit for all this, he argued, was due to American race prejudice. For since whites would not eat in the same restaurants or shop in the same stores as Blacks, Afro-Americans were thereby forced to provide many of these services for themselves. He thought that Afro-Americans still had a long way to go, but they were ahead of any other Black communities he had seen.

In the face of all this Afro-American progress Marcus even blamed West Indians for emigrating rather than standing up and fighting for a better West Indies. He said, "the educated men are immigrating to the United States, Canada, and Europe; the laboring element are to be found by the thousands in Central and South America. These people are leaving their homes simply because they haven't pride and courage enough to stay at home and combat the forces that make them exiles." He now saw Afro-West Indians as people overcome by a great slumber since emancipation. "The Negroes of the West Indies have been sleeping for 78 years," he lamented, "and are still under the spell of Rip Van Winkle. These people want a terrific sensation to awaken them to racial consciousness. We are throwing away good business opportunities in the beautiful islands of the West. We have no banks of our own, no big stores and commercial undertakings; we depend on others as dealers while we remain consumers."

Back to New York

Marcus wound up his nationwide tour in the South. One of his last stops was in New Orleans, Louisiana, which he visited in May 1917. He arrived back in New York with a vast amount of new knowledge and full of confidence. He had visited most of the significant areas of Black population. He had conferred with national and local leaders all over Afro-America. He had carefully read the press and interested himself in the issues of the day as they affected Afro-Americans. He had praised their progress and noted their shortcomings. He was now thinking of leaving the United States in October 1917, but, whether he knew it or not, Afro-America was already growing on him.

Marcus' first speech on his return to Harlem was on June 12, 1917. The occasion was a meeting at the

Bethel AME Church called by Hubert H. Harrison. Harrison was born in St. Croix, Virgin Islands, in 1883 and had emigrated to New York at the age of seventeen. By 1917 he had become one of Harlem's most highly respected intellectuals. His meeting on that June night was to found a new organization, the Liberty League of Negro Americans. There were about 2,000 people present. Marcus stole the show. With a year of constant speaking to Afro-American audiences behind him, he swept the Harlemites off their feet. Most of the people present eventually ended up in the UNIA. Harrison himself later edited the UNIA's newspaper.

Marcus now began holding meetings every Sunday at 3:00 P.M. at Harlem's Lafayette Hall. His talk on July 8, 1917 was entitled "Conspiracy of the East St. Louis Riots" and dealt with a horrible massacre of the Black residents of that city. White mobs had dragged Black men, women and children from tramcars and pounced upon them in the streets. Many were beaten and shot. The mob had then set fire to Black neighbourhoods and shot the victims as they tried to escape from the flames. One newspaper stated—"Negroes are being shot down like rabbits and strung up to telegraph poles." Estimates of the numbers killed ran to as high as over 100. Ten thousand Black survivors fled the city in a single day.

Most of the Blacks killed in East St. Louis were recent immigrants from Louisiana and Marcus had of course only recently returned from there. His speech on this occasion was a bitter one, for he felt deeply for the victims. "The East St. Louis Riots, or rather

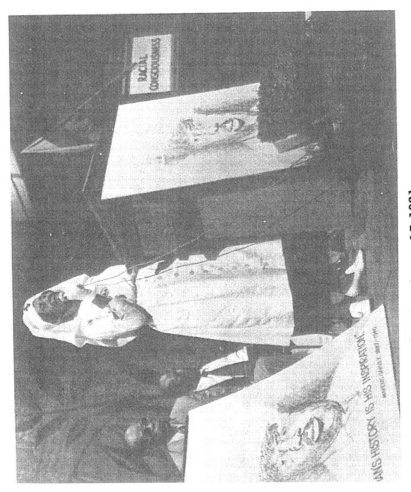

Photo: Tony Martin

Ward Theatre, Kingston, Jamaica, August 17, 1981

massacre, of Monday 2nd," he thundered, "will go down in history as one of the bloodiest outrages against mankind for which any class of people could be held guilty." Voices in the audience shouted "Hear! Hear!" He went on, "This is no time for fine words, but a time to lift one's voice against the savagery of a people who claim to be the dispensers of democracy." The Bible had instructed mankind, he said, that "God created of one blood all nations of men to dwell upon the face of the earth." But yet the Afro-American had always been denied his rights to live in peace. "For three hundred years," Marcus complained, "the Negroes of America have given their life blood to make the Republic the first among the nations of the world, and all along this time, there has never been even one year of justice but on the contrary a continuous round of oppression. At one time it was slavery, at another time lynching and burning, and up to date it is wholesale butchering." Marcus could hardly contain his anger. He denounced the massacre as a "crime against the laws of humanity," a "crime against the laws of the nation," a "crime against nature, and a crime against the God of all mankind." He ended with a word of warning—"white people are taking advantage of Black men today because Black men all over the world are disunited." His audience now erupted into "loud and prolonged cheers." His speech was published in pamphlet form. The proceeds went to a fund for the victims of East St. Louis.

In Harlem Marcus did not confine himself to indoor meetings. Speakers' Corner in London had given him a taste for soapbox oratory. In Harlem speakers regularly addressed crowds on the sidewalks and Marcus followed suit. He set up his soapbox on Lenox Avenue, one of Harlem's busiest streets. He found that his box did not give him as much space to move about and gesticulate as he would have liked. So he had a special step-ladder constructed with a platform on it.

There still remained, however, the task of feeding and clothing himself. So wrapped up was Marcus with his work that he bothered little about the normal comforts of life. He dressed poorly and even shabbily. In a community as fashion-conscious as Harlem he seemed an odd figure. He lived in a cheap, poorly-heated room. His diet also was not particularly inspiring. Someone who knew him well at this time remembered seeing him dine often on corned beef hash in a cheap restaurant. His room, this friend recalled, was liberally stocked with empty cans from which he had eaten many a meagre morsel.

Yet Marcus struggled on. There was an earnestness in his manner which made people stop and listen to him. Besides, he was already acquiring a name for the excellence of his oratory and the power of his voice. Someone who heard him speak from a soapbox at the corner of Lenox Avenue and 135th Street in Harlem said that Garvey could be heard as far away as 125th Street, ten blocks away. This was doubtless an exaggeration, but it made the point. The man had a tremendous voice.

As 1918 approached, Marcus decided to organize a branch of the UNIA in New York. He did not hold office in this branch, since he was still planning to return to Jamaica. Socialist and Republican Party organizers tried to form this UNIA branch into a unit of their respective parties and wrecked it in the process. So Marcus tried again. The same thing happened a second time. This time thirteen of his followers encouraged him to stay and head the New York branch himself. He probably did not require too much persuading by this time, and so the UNIA in New York was off in a big way by 1918. At this point Kingston gave way to Harlem as UNIA headquarters.

5

Garveyism Sweeps The World: 1918-1922

The Universal Negro Improvement Association in New York was legally incorporated on July 2, 1918. It immediately began to spread to other areas. Marcus used the contacts he had established through his many years of travel. He also sent agents over the world spreading his message and organizing branches. Many of those who did this work for him were seamen. He himself continued to travel frequently around the United States and Canada. Whereas his first tour had been to lecture and familiarize himself with North America, now his main purpose was to build the UNIA.

In Harlem the UNIA in due course bought its own meeting place, Liberty Hall, at 120 West 138th Street. UNIA branches all over the world also called their meeting places by the same name.

Ideology

There were many reasons for the rapid growth of the UNIA. Marcus' dedication and tireless work certainly helped. His oratorical skill was a big help, too, for people would come from far and wide just to hear him speak. He also had charisma, the power to attract people and hold their loyalty. He could exert tremendous power over an audience. He could stir their emotions and sweep them along with the power of his words. And the mass of people who became his followers were known for their loyalty. Many thought of him as a superhuman being who had been sent to rescue the race from suffering and oppression. The times were also suitable to the spread of Garvey's message. For the period around the end of World War I was one of ferment in many countries. The war had been fought supposedly to make the world safe for democracy and as it neared its end, oppressed peoples began clamouring for some of that democracy that the politicians had spoken about. The Russian Revolution of 1917 and the Irish Easter uprising of 1916 against the British were, like the formation of the UNIA, part of that worldwide ferment.

This was the time, Marcus thought, for African peoples to make their move. He explained it this way to his followers—"Classes, nations and races which have been quite quiet for centuries are now asserting themselves and demanding a readjustment of things. The despised Negro who has been kicked about and cuffed for over four centuries, and who has been the hewer of wood and the drawer of water for other men, who has merely borne abuse, insult and humiliation for many generations; whose patience, docility and forbearance can only be compared to the prophet

Job, has likewise lifted his bowed head, looking up to God's skies and cried out: 'I am a man and demand a man's chance and a man's treatment in the world.'"

Merely asserting oneself was not enough, however. The oppressed needed a clear body of ideas to guide them in their quest for freedom and equality. Marcus put forward such a set of ideas, "Garveyism," as some people call it. His ideas contained three major elements.

The first was what Marcus called *race first*. He argued that Black people had long been oppressed because of their race. They should therefore strive to put their own racial self-interest first in everything they did. They should support their own businessmen, professionals, writers, athletes and so on, provided that these persons also had their people's interest at heart. Black people, too, should see beauty in their own kind and not try to bleach their skins or otherwise look like what they were not. Marcus also objected to Blacks marrying whites. He saw this as an admission on the part of the Blacks concerned that they were dissatisfied with their own kind. In the days of slavery, he argued, miscegenation or race mixture had occurred because the African woman had no protection from the slave master. That could not be helped now. But there was now no need for Black people to themselves freely continue a practice that smacked so much of slavery.

Race first also meant that Black writers, artists, musicians and dancers should all use their creative talents to help push forward the struggle of their people. Some of the major European writers and poets had used their work to support colonialism and racism and so the writers and poets of the oppressed should not hesitate to side with their own people either. Rudyard Kipling, one of the most celebrated of British poets, was a good example of all this. His widely known poem, "White Man's Burden," written in 1899 when Marcus was a boy, justified the European conquest of darker peoples. Africans and Asians, Kipling wrote, were inferior beings, "half-devil and half-child" and it was the white man's "burden" to catch and civilize them.

The first verse of Kipling's poem read,

> Take up the White Man's Burden—
>   Send forth the best ye breed—
> Go bind your sons to exile
>   To serve your captives' need—
> To wait in heavy harness,
>   On fluttered folk and wild—
> Your new-caught, sullen peoples,
>   Half-devil and half child.

T. Thomas Fortune, one of Afro-America's most famous journalists and an editor of two UNIA newspapers, replied to Kipling in a poem called "The Black Man's Burden." Fortune's first stanza went like this—

> What is the Black Man's Burden,
> Ye hypocrites and vile,
> Ye whited sepulchres
> From th' Amazon to the Nile?

> What is the Black Man's Burden,
> Ye Gentile parasites,
> Who crush and rob your brother
> Of his manhood and his rights?

Marcus applied race first to the writing of history too. He said that "History is written with prejudices, likes and dislikes; and there has never been a white historian who ever wrote with any true love or feeling for the Negro." He pointed out, for example, that Africans built the world's first civilization on the Nile river in what is now Egypt, the Sudan and Ethiopia, but white historians had tried to hide this fact.

Marcus also applied race first to religion. If God was a spirit, he argued, then God had no colour. But it was customary for people to depict their gods in human form and in that case God should be depicted in the race of the people concerned. As far as Marcus was concerned, Africans in the New World were among the very few people anywhere who worshipped gods of a different race and colour from themselves.

In 1921 some churchmen in the UNIA founded the African Orthodox Church. First bishop was the Rev. George Alexander McGuire, formerly an Anglican minister in his native Antigua. The church remained close to the UNIA but was never an official part of it. Marcus did not want to divide his organization along religious lines. Many Muslims also belonged to the UNIA.

The second major idea which Marcus put forward to guide the UNIA was *self-reliance*. He felt that a struggling people should not rely primarily on others for their liberation. A people would not be able to appreciate freedom fully, he thought, unless it learnt to do things for itself. And he felt sure that in the process of making themselves independent and strong, Black people would win the respect of other races. Marcus despised those who felt that they could free their people by begging for help from those who had formerly enslaved them. No one respected a beggar. Black people would cease to be oppressed and discriminated against, Marcus said, when they learnt how to work together to make themselves strong. Achieving this was the purpose he set the UNIA. He once expressed these ideas this way—"If we must have justice we must be strong; if we must be strong we must come together; if we must come together we can only do so through the system of organization."

UNIA branches all over the world tried to be self-reliant in whatever ways they could. They started co-operative businesses, opened schools and agitated for political independence and self-determination.

The third major feature of Marcus' ideology was what he called *nationhood*. By 1918, as we have seen, Liberia and Ethiopia were the only independent Black countries left in the whole world. Marcus felt strongly that Africans the world over would never be really respected until there was a strong Black nation, preferably on the African continent. Such a strong nation could offer economic, diplomatic, military and moral support to Africans, wherever they might be. Marcus knew from his travels that wherever Europeans and North Americans went, their countries' ambassadors and consuls were available to lend a hand in case of emergency. He could find no similar protection for travelling Africans.

Negro Factories Corporation

The Negro Factories Corporation was one of the ways by which the UNIA tried to become self-reliant. It operated a chain of businesses in Harlem. These included restaurants, groceries, launderies, a factory making Black dolls for children, a hat factory, printing press, tailoring establishment, a trucking business and a hotel. The Negro Factories Corporation and other agencies of the UNIA employed over a thousand people around New York in the early 1920s.

Negro World

The *Negro World*, a weekly newspaper, was Marcus' most successful publication. It began in the autumn of 1918 and was published up to 1933. Within a few years it became the most widely distributed Black newspaper in the world. English was its main language but sections were also printed in Spanish and French. The front page of each issue usually carried a stirring message from Marcus Garvey. UNIA members all over the world read and discussed these messages at their weekly meetings, much the same way that Christians read the Gospel at church services on the sabbath.

The British, French and other colonial rulers in Africa and the West Indies were very fearful of the *Negro World*. They did not take kindly to Marcus' preachings of race pride and anti-colonialism. They therefore banned the paper in such places as Trinidad, British Honduras (Belize), British Guiana (Guyana), the Gold Coast (Ghana), Rhodesia (Zimbabwe) and elsewhere, including all the French African colonies. Seamen usually smuggled the paper in wherever it was banned. Persons found with it in these countries were liable to be fined or imprisoned. In Rhodesia (Zimbabwe) in 1927 an African was given life imprisonment for importing a few copies of the *Negro World*. He was later released when protesting Africans took their case all the way to the British parliament.

Marcus told the British that they were wasting their time by trying to suppress his newspaper. Speaking in May 1920 he said, "I think the British Government made a great mistake when they suppressed the *Negro World*, because they only opened the eyes of those sleeping West Indian Negroes to a realization that the government was trying to keep something from them, to keep them in darkness about the great progress of Negroes in the outer world."

Black Star Line

One of the most spectacular events of 1919 came in October that year, when the Black Star Line Steamship Corporation launched its first ship, the *Yarmouth*. The Black Star Line was the brainchild of Marcus Garvey and the UNIA. For Black people to own a modern shipping company at that point in history seemed like an impossible dream to many. White newspapers splashed the news in disbelief all over the world. Black people rejoiced, for this event seemed to provide a ray of hope for their mostly dreary situation.

The Black Star Line was designed to show what self-reliance could do. It was financed with money from its shareholders, all of whom were Black and most of whom were UNIA members. The Line also offered an alternative to the racism practised by white shipping companies. Black passengers were usually segregated in those days. A passenger on the British ship *Maraval,* sailing from Trinidad to New York via Grenada, reported that Black passengers were only allowed to eat after the whites had finished. On the Black Star Line, passengers would be subjected to no such indignities.

It was not easy to find qualified Black officers in 1919 and the Black Star Line was forced to hire some whites, including captains. For its first ship, however, Marcus was able to hire as captain one of the few Black men in the world with the necessary master's licence. This was Captain Joshua Cockburn, a native of the Bahamas who had sailed in Nigerian and other African waters for many years.

It was a proud UNIA which renamed the *Yarmouth,* the *Frederick Douglass,* in honour of the 19th century Afro-American leader. Many thousand Garveyites and UNIA sympathizers turned up at the 135th Street dock in Harlem to witness the ship's launching on October 31, 1919. The *Frederick Douglass* travelled to Cuba, Jamaica and Panama on its first trip. A second and third trip followed, also to West Indian, Central American and United States ports.

The Black Star Line acquired a second vessel, the *Shadyside,* in April 1920. This was an excursion boat and took passengers on summer cruises up and down New York's Hudson River. While anchored for the winter it sank in a snow storm.

The line's third ship was the *Kenawha*, which made its maiden voyage in June 1920. The UNIA renamed this ship the *Antonio Maceo,* after the Black general of Cuba's struggle for independence. In March 1921 the *Antonio Maceo* sailed from New York to Cuba and Jamaica. On its return voyage it broke down and was abandoned near Antilla, Cuba.

A fourth ship was negotiated for but never obtained, even though the company paid down over $20,000.00 on it. The Black Star Line had planned to name this ship after the famous Phillis (often spelt "Phyllis") Wheatley. Wheatley was born in Africa around 1753 and while still a girl was transported to the United States as a slave. She later became one of Afro-America's earliest and most celebrated poets. The company had big plans for the *Phyllis Wheatley.* It was to foster trade between Afro-America, the Caribbean and Africa. Marcus wanted its captain to be Hugh Mulzac, a native of Union Island in the Grenadines near St. Vincent. Mulzac had already served as an officer on the *Frederick Douglass.* During World War II he became the first Afro-American to captain a ship in the United States merchant marine. In 1921 the line hoped to sail the *Phyllis Wheatley* from New York to Monrovia, Liberia via Cuba, the Dominican Republic, St. Kitts, Dominica, Barbados, Trinidad and British Guiana (Guyana).

Everywhere that the Black Star Line ships went they were greeted by scenes of wild enthusiasm. In Havana, Cuba, a Black Star Line vessel was showered with flowers and fruit. In Bocas del Toro, Panama, thousands of workers deserted their jobs for a day to see the *Frederick Douglass*. They brought gifts of flowers and fruit and danced on the ship's decks. In South Carolina, U.S.A., people chartered a special train to take them to the port of Charleston when a Black Star Line ship stopped there.

Yet, the Black Star Line, after its spectacular initial success, failed in the end. The persons, both Black and white, who took part in negotiations for the ships, defrauded the company of tens of thousands of dollars. The white officers also deliberately wrecked the ships' engines, causing thousands of dollars worth of unnecessary repairs. Some of the line's Black employees were also dishonest and stole the company's money.

West Indian Unrest, 1919

The year 1919 was one of much upheaval in the West Indies. Here, too, the World War had awakened people to their awful condition. Here, too, people were impatient with the system governing them and were anxious for a change. At the beginning of the war in 1914, West Indians of all races had rushed to volunteer for military service. Whites were accepted but Blacks were not. The British authorities did not want Afro-West Indians fighting in what some of them referred to as a white man's war. After a while a special force, the British West Indies Regiment, was created for Black West Indians. Though the soldiers were Black, none but whites could be officers. Blacks could rise no higher than sergeant.

The West Indian soldiers were badly treated. They were used mainly as labourers and very few saw any real combat. In 1918 in a place called Taranto in Italy, they were made to clean the latrines of Italian labourers. This was too much for the West Indians to bear and they mutinied, assaulting some white officers in the process. One of the mutineers was executed by the British and many were imprisoned.

Many of these soldiers became ardent Garveyites on their return home. Garvey, in his call for self-reliance, race pride, an end to white colonialism and an independent Black nation, was saying the things that these soldiers felt in their hearts, for the war had made them bitter against their white rulers. Many workers and some of the more politically conscious members of the Black middle class also became Garveyites. The British authorities deported UNIA organizers and burned copies of the *Negro World* when they could, but there was no stopping the spread of Garveyism.

Several colonies erupted into violence in 1919, including Jamaica, Grenada, British Honduras (Belize) and Trinidad and Tobago. In British Honduras one of the leaders of the popular movement was Samuel Haynes, an ex-sergeant of the British West Indies Regiment. In Trinidad a strike by dockworkers early in December 1919 brought the country to a standstill. British troops were called in and several Trinidadians and Tobagonians were killed. The Trinidad Workingmen's Association led the struggle here. Most of its top leaders and many of its members also belonged to the Universal Negro Improvement Association.

First International Convention of the Negro Peoples of the World

By late 1919 Marcus Garvey's name was known throughout the world. The time was now ripe to

begin work on an event every bit as spectacular as the
launching of the Black Star Line had been. Marcus
began planning for a massive assembly which would
bring together representatives of all the world's African peoples. The call went out to UNIA branches and
other organizations all over the world to select delegates for this grand event, the First International Convention of the Negro Peoples of the World.

Marcus' worldwide popularity was now so great
that organizations far and wide answered his call.
Delegates, some of them very prominent members of
their home communities, poured into New York for
the convention, which was held from August 1st to
31st, 1920. From Liberia and South Africa they came,
from England and Canada, from Trinidad and Panama,
and from many other countries. Fully 25,000 Black
people jammed Madison Square Garden to capacity
and overflowed into the surrounding New York streets
for the opening ceremony. No convention in Afro-
American history has ever been bigger, up to the
present day.

The convention parade stretched ten miles, with
delegates marching ten abreast. Marcus rode in an
open car in a military uniform and plumed hat, similar
to the type worn by the leaders of powerful nations
at that time. The UNIA by now had sprouted several
auxiliaries and they added colour to the march. There
were the Universal African Legions, a military outfit
on horseback and on foot. The men and women of
the African Motor Corps, another military auxiliary,
were also on parade. The Black Cross Nurses were
there in their long white dresses, white stockings and

shoes and white headties bearing a black cross. The officers and crew of the Black Star Line were on parade too, in their naval uniforms, and so were the boys and girls of the UNIA Juveniles, the youth arm of the organization. Several brass bands provided music, including the Black Star Line band.

Many of the marchers carried banners proclaiming the ideas and opinions of Garvey. Among them one could see the following—"Africa for Africans;" "All Men Were Created Equal;" "Down With Lynching;" "Toussaint L'Ouverture Was An Abler Soldier Than Napoleon;" and "Negroes Fought in Europe and Can Fight in Africa." After the opening session the convention moved to Liberty Hall in Harlem.

Since African peoples had hardly a nation they could call their own, the UNIA now tried to act as a model of what the future African nation might be. The convention was seen as a parliament of African peoples. The delegates elected Garvey Provisional President of Africa, even as other colonized peoples have always elected provisional governments in exile while fighting for their independence. Garvey also received the title of President General and Administrator of the UNIA. The convention also elected a ceremonial head or potentate. The potentate was the equivalent of a monarch in some countries, or a governor general in others, or a president in those republics where the prime minister is the real head of government. The UNIA potentate was in theory above Garvey, the president general, but only for ceremonial purposes. First potentate was Gabriel Johnson, mayor of Monrovia, Liberia. Twenty-one

high officers were elected in all. Among the other
posts were the Leader of the American Negroes; International Organizer; Surgeon General; Leader of the
Eastern Province of the West Indies, South and Central America; Chaplain General; Auditor General;
Counsel General; Minister of Labour and Industry;
and Minister of the Legions.

Delegates reported to the convention on the problems faced in their home communities. Some from
the African continent were heard in private or used
fictitious names, since they feared victimization when
they returned home. Many of the delegates' grievances were contained in the Declaration of Rights of
the Negro Peoples of the World, adopted midway
through the convention. "Be it Resolved," the document began, "That the Negro people of the world,
through their chosen representatives in convention
assembled in Liberty Hall . . . protest against the
wrongs and injustices they are suffering at the hands
of their white brethren, and state what they deem
their fair and just rights, as well as the treatment they
propose to demand of all men in the future." The
preamble complained of such crimes as lynching in
the United States, noting that "such brutal and inhuman treatment is even practised upon our women."
In the West Indies, it observed, "Negroes are secretly
and cunningly discriminated against, and denied those
fuller rights in government to which white citizens
are appointed, nominated and elected." The preamble
ended with the following forceful statement—"Against
all such inhuman, unchristian and uncivilized treat-

ment we here and now emphatically protest, and invoke the condemnation of all mankind."

The main portion of the declaration contained fifty-four demands. Among them were the following—all persons of African descent anywhere in the world should be accepted as "free citizens of Africa, the Motherland. . . ;" Africans must set out to win justice "by whatsoever means possible;" Blacks must not be tried by all-white judges and juries; use of the word "nigger" must cease; "Negro" must be written with a capital "N;" Black History must be taught to Black children; Blacks must not be excluded from legislative assemblies—there must be no taxation without representation; colonial governments must stop the flogging and whipping of Africans as punishment for crime; the practice of shaving the heads of Black prisoners, and especially women, must be stopped.

With Black women still widely dishonoured and taken advantage of despite the end of slavery, the delegates swore that "With the help of Almighty God, we declare ourselves the sworn protectors of the honor and virtue of our women and children, and pledge our lives for their protection and defense everywhere, and under all circumstances from wrongs and outrages."

The convention also demanded that Blacks must not fight in white wars, except in certain exceptional situations. On a more positive note, the declaration demanded "Africa for the Africans at home and abroad." The colours red, black and green (still very popular today) were declared to be the colours of the

African race and the "Universal Ethiopian Anthem" was adopted as its anthem. Ethiopia here, as in the Bible, referred to Africa in general. The anthem began,

> Ethiopia, thou land of our fathers,
> Thou land where the gods loved to be,
> As storm cloud at night suddenly gathers
> Our armies come rushing to thee.

A total of eight international conventions were held. Five took place in the United States (1920, 1921, 1922, 1924 and 1926). Two took place in Kingston, Jamaica (1929 and 1934). The last one was held in Toronto, Canada, in 1938.

Third World

Only people of African descent were admitted to UNIA membership. But the fact that other persons could not join did not make it a racist organization. This was a period of great national struggles, when colonized and subjugated peoples all over the world were becoming organized for struggle. Mahatma Gandhi, leader of the Indians, first in South Africa and later in India itself, waged a similar struggle. So did Sun Yat Sen of China, who was ably assisted by Eugene Chen, his Trinidad-born foreign minister. Eamon de Valera led a similar struggle of the Irish against the English and in Vietnam, Ho Chi Minh later led a similar fight against first the Japanese, then the French and finally the United States. All of these leaders, like Garvey, were concerned principally, though not only, with their own racial or national group. Garvey differed from the others in that he tried harder to unify his race on a wider international scale. He was also unique in that he operated primarily from a country (the United States) where his people were in a minority and had never had political control.

Garvey and the UNIA were always quick to provide moral support for struggling peoples of other races. On the death of the Russian leader, V. I. Lenin, in 1924, Garvey sent a cable to Moscow praising Lenin for his efforts on behalf of his own people. The *Negro World* was full of articles showing support for the Indian struggle under Gandhi. Garvey also regularly supported the Irish. The Third World leader who had the closest connection to the UNIA, however, was Ho Chi Minh of Vietnam. Ho in his youth had been a seaman and he once spent a few months in New York. The Garvey movement interested him greatly and he regularly attended UNIA meetings.

League of Nations

The League of Nations was a forerunner of the United Nations and was set up in 1919 after the First World War. In his efforts to further the cause of African peoples, Garvey sent several delegations to the League. Germany's African colonies had been taken away by the victorious nations after the World War and Garvey was especially anxious that these colonies should be handed over to Black rule. A UNIA representative had first lobbied for this at the Paris Peace Conference which followed the war in 1919. UNIA delegations put this and other requests to the League of

Nations in 1922, 1923, 1928 and 1931. Garvey himself was the UNIA representative on the last two occasions. The League never agreed to these requests.

Personal Highlights

Marcus went through four major experiences in his personal life between 1918 and 1922. He was almost killed, got himself married, divorced his wife and married a second time.

One day in October 1919 a man walked into the UNIA office and asked to see Marcus Garvey. When Marcus appeared there was a brief conversation before the stranger whipped out a gun and fired four shots. Two of the shots missed Marcus, but one hit him in the head and another got him in the leg. He was rushed to Harlem Hospital where the wounds were happily found to be superficial. The would-be assassin, one George Tyler, was taken to jail but died there under mysterious circumstances. It was widely believed that he had been hired by an influential person or persons to kill Garvey, and that he was himself killed before he could tell his story in court.

Marcus was married not long after this, on December 25, 1919 in Liberty Hall, Harlem. His bride was Amy Ashwood, the seventeen year old girl he had met in Jamaica back in 1914. She had gone off to Panama in 1916 but had come to New York late in 1918. From that period on she had again become very active in the UNIA. Marcus and Amy Ashwood went on a three week honeymoon to Canada, but the marriage was over in less than two months. Marcus accused her of infidelity, dishonesty and various other things. She made similar accusations against Marcus. Marcus divorced Amy Ashwood in June 1922 while she was away in England. One month later he married another Amy, this time Amy Jacques. The two Amys had been best friends from their teenage years in Jamaica and Amy Jacques, wife No. 2, had actually been chief bridesmaid at Amy Ashwood's wedding.

The second marriage lasted until Marcus' death in 1940. It was a successful marriage, despite Marcus' very busy schedule. His work left him with less time for family life than most people have. Amy Jacques proved a perfect spouse for someone in his position. She began her association with Marcus in 1919 as his private secretary. From that point on she immersed herself fully in the work of the organization. She travelled around North America, Europe, Central America and the Caribbean with Marcus on his lecture tours. She was an excellent speaker herself and sometimes addressed UNIA meetings. When Garvey was jailed in the United States (for reasons which will be discussed in Chapter 9), Amy Jacques edited the now famous collection of his articles and speeches which she called *The Philosophy and Opinions of Marcus Garvey, or, Africa for the Africans.* In 1927, with Marcus still in jail, she published two books of his poetry. Amy Jacques also tried her hand at writing essays and short stories. For a time she edited the women's page of the UNIA's weekly newspaper, the *Negro World.* Marcus and Amy Jacques had two sons.

In Harlem the Garveys lived comfortably though modestly in an apartment not far from the UNIA offices. The furnishings included a large number of

books and African art objects. Marcus' sister, Indiana,
and her husband shared the apartment for a short
time. Marcus never owned a car in the United States.
In everyday life he dressed conservatively, even care-
lessly, though on ceremonial occasions it was quite a
different story. For conventions, parades and the like
he could be resplendent in military uniform and
plumed hat, or in the colourful robes of high office.

6

Garveyism In The West Indies And Latin America — 1920s

The West Indies was the birthplace of the UNIA, even as Afro-America was the place which made it a world movement and Africa provided it with its spiritual force. Once the movement got going in the United States, it reached quickly back to the Caribbean. There it had a great impact. A whole generation of trade unionists and political leaders was profoundly influenced by Garveyism, whether they joined the UNIA or not. Meanwhile, emigrating West Indians took the message of Garvey with them as they fanned out across the world. Not only in Latin America and the United States, but in less obvious places such as South Africa and Nigeria, West Indians often cropped up in Garveyite circles.

WEST INDIES

Cuba

Cuba had about 52 UNIA branches in the mid-1920s, more than any other country in the world except for

the United States. A large number of the Cuban UNIA
members were British West Indians and Haitians who
flocked to Cuba in their tens of thousands to cut cane.
Between 1911 and 1921, 22,000 Jamaicans emigrated
to Cuba, making it the second most popular destination for Jamaicans, after the United States. These
emigrants were often treated badly and so they embraced the UNIA with all their might, for it was practically the only organization they could turn to. The
UNIA became their government, friendly society,
social club, political party and even their church. So
great was the influence of the UNIA among these
workers that the British government in 1923 almost
formally recognized the Cuban UNIA as the official
body looking after the interests of British West Indians there. Only the objections of the British governors of Trinidad and Tobago and Barbados prevented
this recognition from taking place.

Since so many of the Cuban Garveyites lived on
and around the sugar plantations, many of the UNIA
branches were named after plantations rather than
after cities, towns or villages, which was the more
normal practice. Still, most of the significant towns
in Cuba contained branches. Among the areas with
UNIA branches were Havana, Antilla Nipe Bay, Banes,
Camaguey, Guantánamo, Sagua la Grande and San-
tiago. Black Star Line ships visited several Cuban
ports and Cuban Garveyites bought many shares in
the company.

In 1921 Garvey made a triumphant tour of Cuba
and was received by President Menocal. During the
world depression which began in the United States in

1929, however, Cuban sentiment turned violently against the British West Indian and Haitian immigrants. Many were killed and mistreated and thousands had to flee back to their home countries. Cuban president Fidel Castro in the 1970s referred to this episode as one of the most disgraceful in Cuban history. In 1920, during this new period of hostility, Garvey was refused permission to land in Cuba. UNIA branches were also closed for several months. Despite the great exodus, however, many of the immigrants remained in Cuba. Many of their descendants still live there, especially in Oriente province. Some are still bilingual (Spanish and English speaking).

Trinidad and Tobago

Trinidad and Tobago had at least 30 UNIA branches, the second highest number in the West Indies and the fourth highest in the world, after the United States, Cuba and Panama. As already mentioned, the Trinidad UNIA was closely allied to the Trinidad Workingmen's Association, for many years the most powerful political force in the country.

The Workingmen's Association was involved in the riots which took place in Trinidad in 1919. The disturbances began among the dockworkers and spread throughout Trinidad and Tobago. The people demanded more pay and better working conditions. They also expressed solidarity with West Indians in Britain who had been attacked by racist mobs during riots there. Most of the leaders and many of the members of the Workingmen's Association belonged to the UNIA and they looked to Garvey for political inspiration.

One Garveyite and Workingmen's Association leader, John Sydney deBourg, was deported to Grenada after the riots, even though he had lived in Trinidad for 37 of his 67 years. The government also banned the *Negro World,* even before the riots. The Trinidad government was, on the whole, one of the most hostile to the UNIA to be found anywhere.

UNIA branches nevertheless spread rapidly all over the country, especially in the south. Some of the places having branches were Port-of-Spain, San Fernando, Balandra Bay, Carapichaima, Caroni, La Brea, Morne Diablo, Princes Town, St. Mary (Moruga), Rio Claro and Siparia.

The hostile central government was controlled by British officials, led by the governor. In the Port-of-Spain City Council, on the other hand, there was a mayor and councillors, all of whom were local people. These had a much more friendly attitude towards the UNIA.

Mayor Alfred Richards and his councillors honoured Marcus with a civic reception when he visited the island in 1937. Richards was the one who had founded the Workingmen's Association forty years earlier, in 1897.

Marcus' staunchest supporter on the Port-of-Spain City Council was Captain A. A. Cipriani, the white deputy mayor and member of the legislative council (central government). Cipriani had himself been mayor several times and had for many years been head of the Trinidad Workingmen's Association. It was Cipriani who encouraged the British-appointed governor, Sir Murchison Fletcher, to allow Marcus

into Trinidad. The British authorities had been thinking of refusing him permission to land because of the
renewed upheaval taking place in Trinidad in 1937.
The workers and peasants, under the leadership of
Tubal Uriah Buzz Butler and others, had been striking
and demonstrating for better living and working conditions and for a more democratic system of government. The British authorities feared that Marcus
would speak on behalf of Butler and the workers.
They therefore allowed him in only on condition that
he make no political speeches. They also prevented
him from addressing any open air meetings. A mammoth meeting planned for Woodford Square, in the
heart of the city, therefore had to be cancelled.

Marcus did speak, however, to indoor audiences
in Port-of-Spain, San Fernando and La Brea. At the
Globe Theatre in Port-of-Spain he met a huge audience which overflowed into the surrounding streets.
Here Captain Cipriani introduced him to the crowd
in a speech filled with lavish praise. Cipriani said, "I
have watched your great and big work and I appreciate the greatness of soul that you have put into
it. . . ." Marcus was equally magnanimous. He explained to the crowd how Cipriani had helped get him
permission to enter the island and he added—"Captain
Cipriani has done me a favour and I shall always re-
member him and thank him for it."

Jamaica

There were eleven branches in Jamaica, Garvey's
birthplace. It must be remembered also that Jamaicans provided large portions of the UNIA membership

in Cuba, Panama, Costa Rica, New York and other places. The Kingston division ran a laundry and a People's Cooperative Bank. Black Star Line ships visited Jamaica and Garvey spent some time there in 1921 while on a tour of the Caribbean and Central America. His activities in Jamaica from 1927 to 1935 will be treated in Chapter 10.

Branches in the mid-1920s were at Bog Walk, Kensington, Kingston, Montego Bay, Morant Bay, Port Antonio, Resource, St. Thomas (Golden Grove), Spanish Town, Swift River and St. Andrew.

British Guiana (Guyana)

There were seven branches here, at Charlestown, Georgetown (2), Lacytown, Parika, Pomeroon and Vergenogen. As in Trinidad, the local UNIA had close ties with the trade union movement, in this case the British Guiana Labour Union (BGLU). At a UNIA meeting in 1921 Hubert Crichlow, leader of the BGLU, heartily endorsed the program of the UNIA. Strong support also came from a local newspaper, the *Daily Chronicle*. The local UNIA's activities included a school. As in the case of Trinidad, the British governor banned the *Negro World* here too. Garvey visited British Guiana during his West Indian tour of 1937.

Dominican Republic

There were six branches in the Dominican Republic, at Barona, La Romana, San Pedro de Macoris, Sanchez, Santo Domingo and Consuela Estate. As in Cuba, many of the members were British West Indian immigrant workers. United States marines, who had been occupying the Dominican Republic since 1915, gave the local UNIA a hard time. In 1921, U.S. military personnel and civil police invaded a UNIA meeting in San Pedro de Macoris and arrested all 15 present, including men, women and children. The marines later suppressed the UNIA altogether for a time and arrested its leaders. Carlos Cooks, who in the 1950s and 1960s led the African Nationalist Pioneer Movement (patterned after the UNIA) in New York, was born in the Dominican Republic. He was the son of a local UNIA organizer.

Barbados

Branches were reported here in Bridgetown (2), Crab Hill (St. Lucy) and Indian Ground (St. Peters). In 1923 the British governor of the island, probably referring to the two Bridgetown branches, said that one was composed of "more solid men" while the other was full of "hot heads." "The Barbadians are generally a quiet well-behaved body of men," he said, "but they are very excitable and easily aroused." The hotheads, he said, had sent threatening letters to planters and were urging workers to strike.

One of the founders of the Barbados UNIA was John Beckles, who later became a highly respected social worker in the island. Other influential Barbadians who either joined the UNIA or maintained close ties with it were Bishop Reginald Barrow, whose son was later prime minister of Barbados and James A. Tudor, whose son was later a deputy prime minister.

On January 3, 1922 John Beckles held an elaborate dinner and dance for UNIA Commissioner, Rev. Richard Hilton Tobitt at his residence, "Beckles Court," St. Lawrence, Christ Church. Tobitt was on a tour of UNIA branches in the Caribbean and South America. Guests arrived to find Beckles Court, in the words of a Barbadian Garveyite, "transformed into a miniature palace, aglow with myriads of vari-coloured electric lights scintillating like fire-flies in the calm of the tropical night." Each course during the dinner was named after some famous figure in African history.

Marcus stopped intransit in Barbados on November 15, 1928 but did not land. He returned for two days in 1937. This time he addressed a mammoth crowd at the steel shed in Queen's Park. James A. Tudor headed the welcoming committee. A sumptuous dinner was held in honour of the distinguished visitor at the Tudor home.

United States Virgin Islands

D. Hamilton Jackson, founder of the St. Croix Labour Union, maintained contact with the UNIA. His brother-in-law, Casper Holstein, was a leader of the Virgin Islands independence movement in New York. Holstein, a wealthy man, also contributed generously to the work of the New York UNIA.

August 31 was an international UNIA holiday and the St. Thomas UNIA's celebration of this event in 1921 was typical of similar celebrations everywhere. There was a big parade complete with brass band, Black Cross Nurses and a delegation from the Virgin

Islands Federation of Labour. The large crowd of on-lookers was treated to many banners bearing slogans such as "Marcus Garvey, the Moses of Our Race." Other banners portrayed African figures mentioned in the Bible, such as Zipporah, the wife of Moses, Candace, the Queen of Ethiopia, and Balkis, the Queen of Sheba. Still others commemorated Caribbean heroes like Toussaint L'Ouverture of Haiti and Edward Wilmot Blyden of St. Thomas, "a son of the soil, [and] the most learned Negro of modern times."

British Honduras (Belize)

The British Honduras UNIA was well-organized, with branches at Belize, Corozal, Stann Creek and Mullins River (Stann Creek). As mentioned earlier, the UNIA figured prominently in the riots of July 1919, which started after white merchants raised prices. Rioters shouted such slogans as, "This is our country and we want to get the white man out. The white man has no right here." One of the leaders of the disturbances was Samuel A. Haynes, a British West Indies Regiment veteran and secretary of the Belize UNIA.

By 1921 the Belize branch was wealthy enough to buy a two storey building for its own Liberty Hall. In that year fourteen of its Black Cross Nurses passed the government examinations and became fully accredited nurses. During 1921 the Belize UNIA also organized a boys' brass band and a choir, mounted an industrial arts exhibition and sent $78.00 to the UNIA headquarters in Harlem. Marcus visited Belize during his Caribbean and Latin American tour of 1921 and was very pleased with what he saw. He was especially impressed by Samuel Haynes and took him back to New York. Haynes played an active role in the organization for many years afterwards.

British governor, Eyre Hutson, banned the *Negro World* from British Honduras in 1919 but he had to admit that it was smuggled in afterwards through Mexico and Guatemala in even greater quantities. Despite all this, he received Marcus during his 1921 visit to the country.

Among the members of the local UNIA was Isaiah Emanuel Morter, a wealthy landowner. Morter visited Marcus in New York and was deeply impressed by the UNIA's efforts. He died in 1924, leaving the greater part of his fortune valued at about $100,000, to the UNIA for its work on behalf of Africa. A local British court held that such a bequest was illegal. The matter dragged on for many years and Garvey's organization never did get the money. Marcus visited British Honduras again in November 1930, this time in connection with the Morter case.

Leeward and Windward Islands

There was a branch of the UNIA in St. Johns, Antigua. Several leaders of the UNIA in the United States came from here. These included the Rev. George Alexander McGuire, the UNIA chaplain general who later founded the African Orthodox Church and George Weston, a one time UNIA leader in New York.

The leader of the Roseau, Dominica branch was J.R. Ralph Casimir, a well-known and influential Garveyite. His poems and articles appeared regularly in the *Negro World.* In 1921 Casimir made a tour of UNIA branches in Trinidad.

Dominica was one of the few islands in which the *Negro World* was never banned. On the other hand, though, the local authorities passed a law forbidding the sending overseas of more than $10.00 in a fort-night. This was to prevent Garveyites buying up too many shares in the Black Star Line.

The UNIA also established itself in Charleston, Nevis and Basseterre, St. Kitts.

In the Windward Islands there were UNIA branches in St. Lucia (Castries), St. Vincent (Stubbs) and Grenada (St. Georges). The UNIA's first anniversary parade in Castries in 1921 attracted some of the largest numbers of spectators ever witnessed there. Only the visit of the Prince of Wales one year earlier rivalled it. And this in spite of the fact that the number of actual marchers was not very large.

St. Vincent was among the many islands which banned the *Negro World* in 1919. The governor, Sir G. B. Haddon-Smith, imposed penalties of six months imprisonment at hard labour and/or a fine of 100 pounds for anyone caught reading Marcus Garvey's newspaper.

A similar attempt to ban the paper in Grenada caused serious protests in 1920. The well-known politician, T. A. Marryshow, opposed the ban and six hundred persons attended a protest meeting in St. Georges. Marryshow supported Garvey from the pages of his *West Indian* newspaper and once published a poem in the *Negro World.*

Marcus visited the Leeward and Windward Islands during his 1937 tour. He was well-received everywhere, although some voices were heard in disagreement with some of his ideas. In Grenada he spoke to an enthusiastic crowd at the Queen's Park pavilion. His subject was "Man's Rise to Greatness."

Other Territories

Suriname (or Dutch Guiana, as it was sometimes called at the time), had one UNIA branch. In 1925 Richard Hilton Tobitt, UNIA high commissioner for the eastern provinces of the West Indies, visited Suriname. The Dutch governor bestowed on him the ceremonial honour of the freedom of the colony. This contrasted sharply with Tobitt's reception in Trinidad, where he was earlier refused permission to land. In the Dutch island of Aruba the UNIA remained active as late as the 1970s. Several of the early UNIA members here came to Aruba from Panama and elsewhere in the Caribbean. Garveyites were also reported in the island of St. Eustatius.

Port au Prince, Haiti, also boasted a UNIA local. Several Haitians also played leading roles in the UNIA in the United States. Elie Garcia was sole UNIA commissioner to Liberia in 1920. In 1919 Eliezer Cadet represented the organization at the Paris Peace Conference, called to settle matters arising from World War I. Jean Joseph Adam was president of the San Francisco UNIA. In 1922 and 1923 he represented the UNIA in its efforts to wrest the German African colonies from the League of Nations at Geneva, Switzerland.

Bermuda rivalled Trinidad for its governmental hostility to the UNIA. Richard Hilton Tobitt, at various times high commissioner to Britain and the eastern provinces of the West Indies, was from Bermuda. He was also an African Methodist Episcopal minister. After he attended the First International Convention of the Negro Peoples of the World in 1920 the government withdrew support for the school which he headmastered.

Needless to say, the *Negro World* was banned in Bermuda. Garvey was also refused permission to land when the ship in which he was travelling stopped here in 1928. He was due to give a speech in Hamilton, where the local branch was located. His wife, Amy Jacques Garvey, had to deliver it instead.

Marcus was treated better in the Bahamas, where there were UNIA branches in Gambier and Nassau. He was allowed in during the 1928 trip. Almost every country in the Caribbean supported at least one UNIA local. This included Puerto Rico, where a single branch existed in San Juan.

CENTRAL AND SOUTH AMERICA
Panama

With 46 branches and a further two in the United States Canal Zone, Panama had the third highest number of UNIA branches in the world. As in Cuba, this fact had a lot to do with the many thousands of British and other West Indians living there. The UNIA played an important role in uniting the immigrants from the various West Indian islands. Prior to the UNIA, Barbadians and Jamaicans especially could not get along. The UNIA, by appealing to the common denominators of race and oppressed condition, largely wiped away petty jealousies and rivalries. In Cuba the organization had brought about a similar unity between Jamaicans and Haitians. Garvey of course was familiar with Panama, having lived there for some time during his travels of 1910 to 1912.

A UNIA delegation visited Panama and the Canal Zone in 1920. The United Fruit Company, a large employer of West Indian labour in Central America, tried to get both governments to ban the delegation. Local Panamanian Blacks as well as the West Indians, together with one Morales, a Spanish Panamanian, threatened to strike on the Panama Canal and burn down the city of Colón. The delegation was allowed to land.

The Colón division ran a bakery and a school with over 300 pupils. In 1928 the Panama UNIA secured the services of a highly respected assistant master from one of Jamaica's top secondary schools, to head a new UNIA secondary school. The intention was to prepare West Indian students in Panama for the same Cambridge exams which students all over the British West Indies took.

Among the areas with UNIA branches were Almirante, Bocas del Toro, Gamboa, Gatun and Panama City.

Costa Rica

There were 23 branches here. Garvey's roots also ran deep in Costa Rica. This had been his first destination after leaving Jamaica in 1910. When he revisited Costa

Rica in 1921 there were scenes of wild jubilation. Fifteen thousand people greeted him at Port Limón. The United Fruit Company had three ships waiting to be loaded with bananas, but the workers were more interested in celebrating Garvey's arrival. The company therefore made a deal. They would provide Garvey with a VIP train to go to San José, the capital, for three days, to provide time for the workers to load the waiting vessels. When the train arrived for Garvey the workers would not let him board the first coach provided, because there were some dirty spots on the outside.

Garvey eventually left for San José, where he was received by the president of Costa Rica. In Port Limón, meanwhile, special trains were put on to bring in Garveyites from outlying areas and a holiday mood reigned for days. The United Fruit Company later provided a launch to take Garvey to Bocas del Toro in Panama.

The Costa Rica UNIA also ran a school. As in Cuba, the UNIA was practically all that the Black population had to look after their needs, and they clung to it. The UNIA is still an important organization in Costa Rica in the 1980s. The *Negro World* was banned here for a while in 1919-1920.

Elsewhere in Central and South America

The UNIA was also firmly entrenched in Honduras, Colombia, Guatemala, Nicaragua, Mexico, Brazil, Ecuador and Venezuela. Many of these were countries Marcus had wandered through between 1910 and 1912.

It is easy to see that many thousands of Garvey-ites were organized throughout the length and breadth of the Caribbean and Central America. Masses of people loved and followed Marcus. Many governmental authorities hated him, especially in the British colonies. The masses loved him because he brought them hope. He taught them to love themselves, to open schools and businesses, to be proud of their heritage and to demand respect. The authorities disliked him because he disturbed the peace of their colonies. He told their subjects not to be content with second class treatment and to fight for equality and justice.

7

Garveyism In Africa — 1920s

Africa occupied a central position in Garvey's thought. His most important goal was to help bring about the day when Africa would expel its European conquerors, unite and become a strong and respected member of the world community of nations. Such a strong Africa would then be able to provide support and protection for African peoples all over the world.

Africa is the world's second largest continent. It is approximately as large as the United States, Europe, China and India all put together. Africa is also one of the world's richest areas in natural resources. It is either the world's chief supplier or one of the more important producers, of gold, diamonds, copper, tin, uranium, petroleum, bauxite and iron ore, to name a few items. The continent also possesses vast potential in agriculture, hydro-electric power and other resources.

Unlike the situation in the Western Hemisphere, Garvey saw that Europeans were still a minority in Africa, despite the great African losses suffered during the slave trade and the scramble for the continent. He therefore argued that Africa was the place where the Black world would have to make a stand. For a strong Africa was the key to a respected African race everywhere. Garvey illustrated his point by the slogan, "A strong man is strong everywhere." He told the story of Jack Johnson, the first Black heavyweight boxing champion of the world. Jack Johnson, he said, was a strong man, and he was strong everywhere he went. He had beaten his white opponents in Australia, he had beaten them in the United States and he could beat them wherever they presented themselves. He was strong, and it did not matter where you took him, he was still strong. The African race, Garvey said, could be like Jack Johnson. If it became strong in Africa, then it would be strong everywhere.

Despite their sufferings during slavery and afterwards, many Africans in the western world had picked up skills which would be useful in the task of rebuilding Africa. Garvey said that it was their duty to take these skills back to Africa. He therefore encouraged energetic and well-qualified Afro-Americans and West Indians to return and make a contribution to the African continent. Afro-Americans especially should look towards Africa, he thought. For they were such a small minority in the United States, and their oppression was so severe, that he feared they might be wiped out at some stage, even as the Caribs and Arawaks of the West Indies, and the Red

Indians of North America, had been wiped out by the conquering Europeans.

Garvey planned to make an African tour in 1923. When the British government heard of his plans they became so alarmed that they instructed the governors of their African colonies not to let him land if he should arrive at any of their ports. Garvey died without ever setting foot in Africa, but his impact there was tremendous all the same.

Southern Africa

There were more UNIA branches in South Africa than anywhere else on the continent. Branches were located in Cape Town, Claremont (Cape), Woodstock (Cape Town), Evaton (or New Clare, Johannesburg), Goodwood, Pretoria and East London. In addition, Garveyites were in the leadership of the two most powerful African organizations in South Africa, namely the Industrial and Commercial Workers Union (normally known as the ICU) and the African National Congress (ANC). The president of the ICU from 1924 to 1929 was J. G. Gumbs, who was originally from the West Indies. Gumbs was also a trustee of the Cape Town UNIA. Several ANC leaders were also great admirers of Marcus Garvey and they spread his message in their newspapers. One such was James Thaele, president of the Cape Western ANC.

In South Africa at that time some African Christians had broken away from white missionaries and had established independent congregations known as "Ethiopian" churches. Some of these adopted Garvey as a prophet who, like Moses, had come to free his people from bondage.

The *Negro World* was not actually banned in South Africa but its agents were sometimes assaulted and harassed.

The local UNIA branch in Basutoland (now the independent nation of Lesotho), was one of the largest in Africa. It reported attendances of 500 and 600 at meetings in 1926. Lesotho was at the time a British colony and was (and still is) completely surrounded by South Africa.

There were also UNIA branches at Luderitz and Windhoek in South West Africa (Namibia). One can still (in the 1980s) hear UNIA songs sung by old people in Namibia.

There is no record of a UNIA branch in Bechuanaland (Botswana) or in Swaziland, but interest in Garvey was reported among local inhabitants in both places. Swaziland, like Lesotho, is a land-locked country, being surrounded by South Africa and Mozambique. The King of Swaziland once told Garvey's first wife, Amy Ashwood Garvey, that he had heard of only two Afro-Americans, namely Jack Johnson the boxer and Marcus Garvey.

Liberia

Liberia had a special attraction for Garvey. It had been established in 1820 for Afro-American ex-slaves who wanted to return. Over the years it had maintained this special relationship with Africans in the western world. It was also independent (since 1847) and one of the nearest African countries to the United

States and the Caribbean.

Garvey hoped to move the UNIA headquarters and several thousand of his followers to Liberia. His first move was in 1920 when he sent Haitian Elie Garcia as sole commissioner on a mission to Liberia. Garcia met with high government officials and outlined the UNIA's plan. The Liberians gave him every encouragement. He however wrote a secret report for Garvey, which criticized some aspects of Liberia. He found the Liberian ruling class to be lazy and incompetent. Nor did he like the way the descendants of slaves from the Western Hemisphere lorded it over the native-born Africans. He advised that when the UNIA got a foothold in the country it should right these wrongs. This report later found its way into the hands of the Liberian government and it helped turn them away from Garvey.

At the First International Convention of the Negro Peoples of the World held later in 1920, Gabriel Johnson, mayor of Monrovia, Liberia's capital city, was elected potentate or ceremonial head of the UNIA. Then in 1921 the UNIA set up a small embassy in Monrovia and sent over a group of experts to begin work on a UNIA settlement. They included persons skilled in pharmacy, construction, agriculture and other useful subjects. Eventually, in 1924, after the visit of a high-powered UNIA delegation, the Liberian government called a halt to the UNIA's plans. By that time a UNIA sawmill and other expensive equipment was on the way to Liberia. The organization lost thousands of dollars as a result of all this.

The main reasons for the Liberian action were (1) fear that Garvey would use his great popularity in Liberia to win political power from the ruling group; (2) pressure from the French and British governments, whose colonies bordered Liberia—they did not want any UNIA headquarters so near to their African subjects; (3) pressure from the United States government— the Firestone Rubber Tire Company of the U.S.A. soon afterwards obtained one million acres to grow rubber trees, including some of the land promised to Garvey; (4) the influence of Garvey's Afro-American rival, W.E.B. DuBois, who visited Liberia early in 1924 as a special representative of the United States government. (See Chapter 9 for more on Garvey's Black rivals).

There was a UNIA branch in Monrovia. It was still operating in the 1970s. Many individual Garveyites emigrated to Liberia over the years, in spite of the ban on the UNIA.

British West Africa

Lagos, the Nigerian capital, contained several hundred UNIA members in 1920. A branch was also started in the northern city of Kano. The Black Star Line had an office in Lagos.

Some of Nigeria's outstanding politicians in the struggle for independence either belonged to the Lagos UNIA or were influenced by Garvey. One of them was Nnamdi Azikiwe, who in 1960 became the first governor general of independent Nigeria. While still a schoolboy in 1920 a friend showed him a battered copy of the *Negro World*. Some of the pages were no longer legible, but what was still easy to

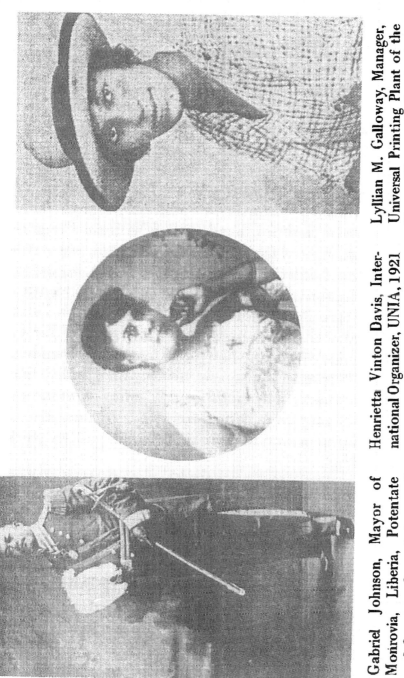

Lyllian M. Galloway, Manager, Universal Printing Plant of the Negro Factories Corporation, 1922

Henrietta Vinton Davis, International Organizer, UNIA, 1921

Gabriel Johnson, Mayor of Monrovia, Liberia, Potentate and Supreme Commissioner of the UNIA, 1921

read was Garvey's front page message, written in big, bold type. Garvey won him over immediately. Azi-kiwe said many years later in his autobiography that "Marcus Garvey's motto [One God! One Aim! One Destiny!] gave the ambitions to be of service for the redemption of Africa."

The UNIA was active in the Gold Coast (now Ghana) as early as 1919. There were branches in Accra and Amanpupong. As in Nigeria and South Africa, Garvey influenced political figures here. J. E. Casely Hayford, head of the National Congress of British West Africa, praised Garvey in his news-paper, the *Gold Coast Leader.* The UNIA honoured Casely Hayford at its Third International Convention of the Negro Peoples of the World in Harlem in 1922.

Another Ghanaian politician influenced by Garvey was Kwame Nkrumah, first president of independent Ghana. Nkrumah wrote in his autobiography that Garvey's book, *The Philosophy and Opinions of Marcus Garvey, or, Africa for the Africans,* had a greater influence on his thinking than any other work he ever read.

From Sierra Leone came George O. Marke, dep-uty potentate of the UNIA. He was a former town clerk of Freetown and a past student of Oxford Uni-versity. There were UNIA branches at New Hope, Freetown and West Ward.

The Gambia completed the list of British West African colonies. UNIA activity was reported from here in the early 1920s, though the surviving UNIA files do not list a branch.

By 1923 the *Negro World* was banned throughout the four territories of British West Africa.

British East Africa

Harry Thuku, major Kenyan nationalist in the 1920s, corresponded with Marcus Garvey. Jomo Kenyatta, a disciple of Thuku and later first president of independent Kenya, considered himself a Garveyite at this time. He recalled how someone who could understand English would read Garvey's *Negro World* message to a group of Africans who would memorize it and spread the message far and wide across the countryside.

Bishop George Alexander McGuire's African Orthodox Church spread to Kenya and has remained an important denomination there.

Reuben Spartas Mukasa, a Ugandan admirer of Garvey, brought the Orthodox Church to that country in 1929. Godfrey Binaisa, president of Uganda for a short period in 1980, recalls being familiar with Garvey's *Black Man* magazine in his youth, even though it was banned in Uganda.

Ethiopia was the other independent African country in the 1920s. Unlike Liberia, which was reasonably easy to get to, Ethiopia, over on the eastern side of Africa, was a long and tiring journey away from Afro-America and the Caribbean. Yet several Garveyites emigrated there from 1930 onwards. They were led by Barbados-born Arnold J. Ford, who had been musical director of the UNIA. The connections between Ethiopia, Rastafarians and the Garvey movement will be discussed in Chapter 10.

British Central Africa

Surviving UNIA records do not indicate any branches in Nyasaland (Malawi), Northern Rhodesia (Zambia),

or Southern Rhodesia (Zimbabwe). However, there
was interest in Garvey in all these places. In 1920 the
British authorities expressed concern about Garvey-
ites from Nyasaland (Malawi) who were then living in
New York. In 1923 the *Negro World* was banned in
Nyasaland (Malawi) and Northern Rhodesia (Zambia).
As already mentioned, a Nyasalander was in 1927
sentenced to life imprisonment in Southern Rhodesia
(Zimbabwe) for importing a few copies of the *Negro
World*.

Belgian Congo (Zaire)

The Belgian administration here was one of the most
cruel and oppressive in the whole of colonized Africa.
Yet even the Belgians could not totally prevent the
entry of Garveyite influences. In the 1920s there was
a nationalist religious movement led by Simon Kimbangu, who the Belgians accused of being inspired
by Garveyism. Several UNIA organizers from Sierra
Leone and the Gold Coast (Ghana) were deported
from the Belgian Congo for spreading the word there.
The Belgians confiscated letters addressed to local
residents from the Black Star Line.

French Africa

The *Negro World* was banned throughout the French
African colonies. In Senegal in 1922 UNIA branches
were reported from Dakar, Rufisque and Thies.
Sierra Leone Garveyites living in Senegal were deported.
    Prince Kojo Tovalou Houénou of Dahomey was a
guest at the UNIA's 1924 international convention in

Harlem. He lived in Paris but is said to have led an unsuccessful Garveyite uprising in Dahomey in 1925.

Portuguese Africa

Members of the Liga Africana, a group of conservative Africans living in Portugal, were heckled in the Portuguese territories when they tried to speak against Garveyism. In 1924, however, a UNIA delegation on its way to Liberia held talks with the Liga Africana in Lisbon, Portugal. The main Portuguese colonies in Africa were Angola, Mozambique, Guinea-Bissau and the Cape Verde Islands.

8

Garveyism In North America, Europe And Australia — 1920s

North America was far and away the largest stronghold of Garveyism. There were well over 700 UNIA branches in Afro-America alone, or roughly two-thirds of all the branches in the world. The state of Louisiana had seventy-four branches, one and a half times as many as Cuba, which led the rest of the world with fifty-two branches.

Afro-America

New York City, the home of Harlem and the UNIA headquarters, boasted a UNIA membership of some 35,000 persons at its peak. This made it by far the largest branch in the world. Marcus was the main attraction and he could be heard weekly at Liberty Hall, when he was not away on tour. Crowds of 5,000 and more were not unusual for regular Sunday evening meetings at Liberty Hall. New York was also the home of the Black Star Line, the *Negro World*, the

96

businesses of the Negro Factories Corporation and the venue for the early international conventions.

Among the northeastern states Pennsylvania had 45 branches; New Jersey, 31; New York State, 16; Connecticut, 10; Massachusetts, 7; and Rhode Island, 2. Apart from New York, some of the country's largest branches were in this area, in cities such as Pittsburgh and Philadelphia in Pennsylvania and Boston in Massachusetts.

The larger branches here, as in other parts of the country, owned considerable amounts of property. In the 1920s Philadelphia owned real estate valued at $20,000. Pittsburgh owned $30,000 worth.

The Mid-West, like the Northeast, contained large communities of recent immigrants from the South. There were 39 UNIA branches in Ohio; 23 in Illinois; 21 in Missouri; 14 in Michigan; 13 in Indiana; 7 in Kansas; 3 in Colorado; 2 in Iowa; and one each in Nebraska, Utah and Wisconsin.

Several of the world's largest branches were in this region too, especially in large cities like Youngstown and Cleveland in Ohio; Chicago, Illinois; Detroit, Michigan; and Gary, Indiana. In 1927 the Detroit UNIA owned property worth $50,000 and the Chicago branch, $30,000.

Southern states tended to have more branches than anywhere else. There were several reasons for this. First, the vast majority of Afro-Americans in the 1920s still lived in the South, despite the large exodus to northern cities. Secondly, in the South the need for the UNIA was probably greatest. The UNIA often spread most widely where oppression was harshest. This may help explain why the South had most branches in the United States, Cuba had the most in the West Indies and South Africa led in Africa.

As in other places, the UNIA spread, not only in the cities, but all over the country areas. There were a few very large single branches here, notably in New Orleans, Louisiana. There were 74 branches in Louisiana; 48 in Virginia; 47 in North Carolina; 44 in West Virginia; 44 in Mississippi; 38 in Arkansas; 32 in Florida; 28 in Oklahoma; 26 in Georgia ; 24 in South Carolina; 11 in Alabama; 10 in Maryland; 9 each in Tennessee and Texas; 8 in Kentucky; 3 in Delaware; and 2 in the District of Columbia.

Western states had relatively fewer Black people, except for California. There were 16 branches in California; 4 in Arizona; 3 in Washington State; and 1 in Oregon.

Canada

Some of the earliest UNIA branches were located in Canada. Those in Montreal and Toronto are still (in the 1980s), very much in existence. Garvey honeymooned in Ottawa, Toronto and Montreal in 1919 and 1920. After the break-up of that first marriage his wife, Amy Ashwood Garvey, returned to Montreal for a while.

The UNIA's fifteen branches in Canada were spread across the country, from Vancouver, British Colombia in the West to Sydney, Nova Scotia in the East. There had been Black people in Canada for a long time. Some Jamaican maroons were banished there in the late 18th century and Afro-Americans fled there during slavery times. In the early 20th century West Indian workers and students found their way there.

Europe

England's Black population was still small in the 1920s, but the UNIA nevertheless established itself in London and Manchester. There were two branches in Wales, at Barry Dock and Cardiff. Garvey established ties also with the Black community in France. He visited both Britain and France on various occasions.

Australia

The Sydney, Australia UNIA branch was undoubtedly the furthest from Harlem. It illustrated how, in those days before commercial air travel and television, and before even the widespread use of radio, Garvey and the UNIA were nevertheless able to draw communities from practically all over the world together into a single organization with a single aim.

9

Enemies Within And Without

By the early 1920s it was clear to all who had eyes to
see that the Garvey movement was the biggest and
most powerful organization of its kind in history.
Others had dreamed before of uniting Africans the
world over into one vast organization, but none had
succeeded the way Marcus had. The UNIA was truly a
provisional nation, as Marcus called it. It had a ceremonial head in its potentate, an executive head in
Marcus, an industrial sector, the beginnings of an
army, a small diplomatic service, ample financial resources, its own media and a worldwide membership.
The one thing it lacked, which every nation needs,
was an area of land where it could set up an independent government. That is why Garvey wanted to
move his headquarters to Liberia, the only easily
accessible place in Africa at the time.

Marcus' very success turned out to be a big problem, for it attracted the hostility of nations, organi-

zations and individuals who, for various reasons, felt threatened by his success. These included the British and United States governments, the Communist International and certain Black leaders who disagreed with his philosophy.

Great Britain

Many millions of the people who Marcus organized, influenced and struggled for, were the colonized subjects of Britain. And it was not in Britain's interest to encourage people who desired to be free of colonialism. Much of the British hostility to the UNIA has already been seen. British governors and their agents banned the *Negro World* in their African and West Indian colonies, jailed and deported Garveyites and denied them entry into some countries. Even in independent countries like Costa Rica, South Africa, Panama, Liberia and the United States, British diplomats spied on the UNIA and sometimes encouraged the local authorities to move against it. In New York, for example, the British consul general in 1923 got together with some anti-Garvey West Indians to publish the *British West Indian Review*. The purpose of this magazine was to counteract Garvey's message and stimulate loyalty to the British king and country.

United States

The United States government did not like Garvey's activities either. From as early as 1917, undercover police began watching his movements. Marcus said that George Tyler, the man who tried to kill him in 1919, announced that he had been sent by Edwin P.

Kilroe, an assistant district attorney who had given Marcus some trouble.

From 1919 the U.S. officials began looking for a way to deport him, but they needed a suitable pretext, and it was a few more years before they found one. Meanwhile in 1921 Marcus left the United States for a short tour of the West Indies and Central America. He almost did not make it back, for United States embassies and consulates refused to give him a reentry visa. It was five months before he managed to get back in. He was detained by the immigration authorities when he arrived in New Orleans but they eventually let him go after he sent telegrams to the United States president and secretary of state.

Marcus and the UNIA were harassed in various other ways. The authorities liked to arrest him every year in the middle of his international conventions. The charges usually came to nothing. Liberty Halls were sometimes raided by police for one reason or another. People were killed during at least one such raid. Some influential North American newspapers were also very hostile to the UNIA and alternated between attacking Marcus and making fun of him.

Communists

The earliest communist parties in the U.S.A. were founded in 1919, just as Marcus was taking off into world prominence. Communist parties everywhere have as a high priority the championing of the cause of workers and peasants. Those in the United States were no exception. Throughout the 1920s, however, they failed to attract any significant number of Black workers and peasants, or any other Black persons for that matter. The UNIA on the other hand had more Black workers and peasants in it than any other political organization in the United States.

The communists therefore figured that in order to get to the Black masses they would have to find some way into or around the UNIA. Throughout the 1920s they refused to leave Garvey alone. UNIA international conventions were always open to fraternal delegates from other organizations and so in 1921, the communist-dominated African Blood Brotherhood sent some representatives to attend. These Black communists then brought in a white woman to address the convention. She told them that Russia, like the UNIA, desired a free Africa. The UNIA, she said, would be welcome in Moscow. She then called on Marcus to come out in support of the communist program, but he politely declined to commit himself. He had no especial hostility towards the communist program, and he praised the Russian revolutionary leaders, V.I. Lenin and Leon Trotsky. But he felt strongly that Africans should be a strong, self-reliant force in the world and not merely an appendage to someone else's struggle.

Communists believed that class was more important than race. Therefore Afro-American workers should unite with white workers first, rather than with other Blacks on the basis of race. Garvey felt that in a racist country, even white workers were so infected with racism that it would be a long time before Blacks could meaningfully unite with them merely on the basis of a similar class background. He pointed out that most lynch mobs were composed of white workers. White United States workers at that time also largely prevented Black workers from joining their trade unions.

The Communist Party of the U.S.A. made many other attempts to woo Garvey or entice away his followers. At times when these attempts failed they became frustrated and attacked him bitterly. Communist newspapers and magazines, both in the United States and in other countries, were full of such attacks. They liked to call him names like "faker" and "misleader." Communists and Garveyites also fought each other on the streets of Harlem.

The struggle between Garveyites and communists reached other countries too, since both the UNIA and the Communist International (world communist movement) existed around the globe. In South Africa Garveyites drove communists out of the leadership of the Industrial and Commercial Workers Union.

Enemies Within

Marcus was sure that the United States government planted spies in his organization. In addition, there were those who could not resist the temptation to steal. Millions of dollars passed through the UNIA and its subsidiaries, like the Black Star Line and the Negro Factories Corporation. Dishonest employees siphoned off some of this money. Several of these employees were brought before the courts by the UNIA but they were often dealt with leniently, for the courts were not particularly fond of Marcus Garvey. Commenting on the enemies within, Marcus said, "In the fight to reach the top the oppressed have always been encumbered by the traitors of their own race, made up of those of little faith and those who are generally susceptible to bribery for the selling out of the rights of their own people."

There was also the problem of disgruntled former UNIA members and employees who had been expelled from the organization or dismissed from their jobs for one reason or another. These sometimes tried to sabotage Garvey's efforts. One of the most dangerous was Samuel Augustus Duncan, a United States immigrant from St. Kitts. Duncan had been president of one of the early attempts to set up a New York UNIA branch in 1918. He had fallen out with Marcus after the latter's refusal to have the UNIA turned into an auxiliary of a political party. In 1920 Duncan wrote the governors of the British West Indian and African colonies as well as the South African authorities. He told them that the UNIA was "not only anti-white and anti-British but was engaged in the most destructive and pernicious propaganda to create disturbance between white and colored people in the British possessions." Agents, he said, had left the United States to quietly spread Garveyism in the West Indies. Duncan finally suggested that the British authorities should, in "the cause of empire," check out very carefully any Black persons entering their colonies from the United States or the Panama Canal. Such persons might well be Garveyites.

The British took Duncan's letter very seriously. Their consul general in New York refused passports to all British West Indians wishing to visit their home-

lands unless they first denounced Garvey. The South
Africans, too, placed a ban on Afro-Americans and
Afro-West Indians wishing to enter that country.

Integrationists

Marcus, in his emphasis on race first, self-reliance and
nationhood, and in his concern for Africa, belonged
to a school of thought which over the years had come
to be known as Black nationalism. The traditional
rivals of the Black nationalists, especially in Afro-
America, were the integrationists. Afro-American
integrationists believed that their destiny was bound
up in the United States. Their main goal was to try
and win acceptance by white Americans and to enter
the mainstream of United States life. Unlike Marcus,
whose UNIA was restricted to persons of African descent, the integrationists preferred to work in interracial organizations. Unlike Marcus, they were not
preoccupied with any thoughts about a Black nation
in Africa. They wanted to be part of an integrated
nation in North America.

There were several integrationist organizations,
the most powerful of which was the National Association for the Advancement of Coloured People
(NAACP). This was formed in 1909 by liberal white
people. Most of its national executive when Marcus
arrived in the United States was white. Its major
Black spokesman was Dr. W.E.B. DuBois, one of
Afro-America's most famous scholars.

The integrationists were a powerful group. They
owned many Black newspapers and often had the ear
of influential whites in government, publishing and

other areas. They waged a relentless campaign against
Marcus Garvey and the UNIA. They disliked Garvey
for the differences in ideology stated above and for
other reasons too. One thing they did not like was his
style. He struck them as a rabble rouser, appealing as
he did directly to the poor and often less well-edu-
cated masses. They were used to quieter, more genteel
behaviour. And Garvey wore a military uniform and a
plumed hat on his parades. They could not stomach
that. It seemed to them that the man was making a
fool of himself. Yet they did not mind when European presidents, governors and diplomats wore simi-
larly colourful attire. They themselves sported flashy
costumes on the parades for their fraternal organizations and secret societies.

More importantly, Garvey's success seemed to
show up their own inability to mobilize the mass of
Afro-Americans. They could not understand how
come a man who had arrived penniless in the United
States in 1916, could launch a Black Star Line in
1919, even though he refused to accept money from
whites. They had less to show for the white philan-
thropy they received. They also could not understand
how such a man, within four short years of his arrival,
could assemble 25,000 people in Madison Square
Garden.

Even though some of the integrationists were
interested in Africa, that continent was nowhere near
the top of their list of priorities. They thought that
Marcus was wasting his time trying to establish the
UNIA in Africa. For they were optimistic that racial
discrimination in the United States would end in

Capt. James Thornhill of Harlem, one-time bodyguard of Marcus Garvey —
Garvey birthday celebrations, St. Ann's Bay, Jamaica, August 16, 1981

Photo: Tony Martin

another fifty years or so. Marcus, on the other hand, feared that in a century or two, Afro-Americans might be wiped out if they were not careful.

Two prominent integrationists actually made fun of Marcus because of his colour and physical features. W.E.B. DuBois described him as "A little, fat black man, ugly, but with intelligent eyes and a big head. . . ." Rev. Robert W. Bagnall, a high-ranking Black NAACP official, called him "A Jamaican Negro of unmixed stock, squat, stocky, fat and sleek with protruding jaws, and heavy jowls, small bright pig-like eyes and rather bulldog-like face."

The integrationist press attacked Marcus bitterly, month in and month out. The *Negro World* replied in equal measure. Garvey's *Negro World* reply to DuBois' insults, for example, was headlined, "W.E. BURG-HARDT DU BOIS AS A HATER OF DARK PEOPLE: Calls His Own Race 'Black and Ugly,' Judging From the White Man's Standard of Beauty."

In 1922 the integrationists launched a fierce campaign entitled, "Marcus Garvey Must Go!!!" They held public meetings and distributed leaflets denouncing Marcus, all over the United States and Canada. In January 1923 eight of their leaders wrote the attorney general of the United States calling for Garvey's arrest and deportation. Their letter, and their campaign generally, influenced the government which was at the time getting ready to prosecute Garvey for alleged mail fraud.

Trial, Imprisonment and Deportation

The Marcus Garvey Must Go campaign began after Marcus was charged by the United States with using the mails to defraud, but before the matter went to court.

The campaign did great damage to his chances of a fair trial. The letter of the eight to the attorney general had made no bones about their desire to see Garvey convicted. "The UNIA," the eight wrote, "is composed chiefly of the most primitive and ignorant element of West Indian and American Negroes." They called upon the attorney general to break up the UNIA and convict its leader.

Marcus called this letter "the greatest bit of treachery and wickedness that any group of Negroes could be capable of." "Like the good old darkey," he said, "they believe they have some news to tell and they are telling it for all it is worth. . . ."

The trial of Marcus Garvey took place in 1923 and lasted for a month. The judge, Julian Mack, admitted that he was a member of the NAACP but still insisted on trying the case. The NAACP was of course deeply involved in the Marcus Garvey Must Go effort.

Three other Black Star Line officials were indicted along with Marcus, but as the trial progressed it became evident that Marcus himself was the only defendant that the government wished earnestly to see behind bars. To add to his problems, Marcus dismissed his lawyer early on. He claimed that his lawyer had worked out a deal with the judge whereby Marcus would plead guilty and hope for a light sentence. Thereafter Marcus acted as his own lawyer. But he was no lawyer, and probably hurt his case by trying to play lawyer before a white judge, prosecutor and jury, some or all of whom may have been prejudiced against him from the start.

The government's case was that Marcus Garvey, as president of the Black Star Line, was responsible for circulars and advertisements claiming that the line was sure to make a profit. The line, of course, eventually folded. The government sought to prove that Marcus knowingly misled shareholders into expecting profits when he knew that there would not be any.

Marcus argued that companies fail every day and the fact that they all promise profits does not make them fraudulent. He tried to show how some of his subordinates had deliberately sabotaged the ships and stolen huge sums of money. Without this thievery and sabotage the line might well have been able to pay dividends. One or two former employees, including Captain Joshua Cockburn, even admitted their dishonest acts.

When it came to proving that Marcus had actually been responsible for sending fraudulent circulars through the mail, the government could do no better than produce an empty envelope bearing a Black Star Line stamp and addressed to a former shareholder. The court simply presumed that the envelope was authentic and that certain circulars had been in it.

The result of the trial was a conviction for Marcus and acquittal for his three co-defendants. The prosecutor showed his lack of interest in the co-defendants in his address to the jury. He asked them, "Gentlemen, will you let the tiger loose?" The tiger was Garvey. The prosecutor seemed momentarily to forget that there were other defendants in the case.

Judge Mack, who had clashed with Marcus throughout the long trial, ended matters by imposing the maximum imprisonment of five years, plus the maximum fine of $1,000, plus the entire costs of the case. But that was not all. Even though he appealed, Marcus was kept in jail for three months before being granted bail.

As the police vehicle bore him to jail at the end of the trial, several hundred of his supporters created a scene outside the courthouse. They prayed and lamented and some tried to block the vehicle. There was a lot of wild talk in the newspapers about the Universal African Legions planning some military action to free Garvey, but nothing of the sort took place. At one point during the trial the judge had stopped proceedings to try Charles Lennon, a Garveyite who was accused of threatening prosecution witnesses. Lennon protested his innocence but was sentenced to two months in jail.

When Marcus was finally released on bail, his supporters showed their confidence in him by putting up enough money to launch a new shipping line, the Black Cross Navigation and Trading Company. This line purchased the *General Goethals*, which it renamed the *Booker T. Washington*. This ship was christened in January 1925 and journeyed to Cuba, Jamaica and Panama. Marcus lost his appeal and was jailed in February 1925 and the ship had to be sold to pay debts on its return to New York.

Marcus was imprisoned at Atlanta penitentiary. UNIA members and many non-members too, immediately launched a massive worldwide effort to secure his release. Telegrams, letters and petitions bearing hundreds of thousands of signatures poured into various United States government departments. Churches regularly held "Marcus Garvey Sundays." In South Africa the African National Congress called for his release. In Moscow the International Peasants' Council did likewise. In Harlem 150,000 people turned out for a demonstration and rally demanding the UNIA leader's release.

Jamaicans celebrated a "Garvey Release Week" in 1927. There were open air meetings as well as large indoor meetings at the Kingston Liberty Hall (76 King Street) and the Ward Theatre. H.A.L. Simpson, a member of the Kingston and St. Andrew Corporation Council, drafted a petition which was sent off to the president of the United States. Simpson had been one of Garvey's fellow members of the National Club in 1909. He later became a member of the legislative council and mayor of the corporate area.

In jail meanwhile, Marcus consoled himself by writing two books of poems, *The Tragedy of White Injustice* and *Selections from the Poetic Meditations of Marcus Garvey*. He also tried to hold together his organization, but schisms appeared, especially at headquarters in New York, as various factions began to struggle for power in their leader's absence.

The clamour for Garvey's release eventually became so insistent that in November 1927 President Calvin Coolidge commuted the sentence to take effect immediately. The authorities deported him, however, in a move that may have been illegal. They did not even allow him a few days in New York to

straighten out his affairs. He was taken to the port of
New Orleans and shipped off to Jamaica via Panama.
Five thousand of his supporters gathered in the rain
at the dock on December 2, 1927 to see him off.
Marcus addressed them from the deck of the *Saramacca*. He said, "I was convicted not because anyone
was defrauded in the temporary failure of the Black
Star Line, brought about by others, but because I
talked about Africa and about its redemption. . . ."
He asked his followers to keep the faith and he promised to continue his life's work. "I live and die for
Africa redeemed," he said. "The greatest work is yet
to be done. I shall with God's help do it."

The crowd sang the UNIA hymn, "God Bless Our
President," as the *Saramacca* bore their leader away
from those United States, where he had achieved a
glory not often matched and where his suffering had
likewise been great.

Marcus Garvey never set foot in the United States
again. The nearest he came to revisiting his old stomp-
ing ground was in 1937, when a ship in which he was
travelling from Canada to the West Indies stopped at
Boston. A delegation of local Garveyites came on
board, but he was not permitted to leave the ship.

10

Back To Jamaica: 1927-1935

A Hero's Welcome

Several days out of New Orleans the *Saramacca* stopped at Cristobal, United States Canal Zone. As at New Orleans, the local Black population demonstrated their heartfelt appreciation for all that Marcus had done. All the silver employees (Black workers) on the docks raised their hats to Marcus in a spontaneous gesture of solidarity and respect. Marcus returned the compliment. He was not allowed to land in this United States possession, where the Black populace had hoped to greet him in grand style. Local Garveyites had however obtained permission from the governor of the Canal Zone to send aboard a six member delegation representing Canal Zone and PanamaUNIA members. No other Garveyites were allowed inside the pier gates. A reporter noted that Marcus was affable "and the delegation which waited on him, standing stiffly and slightly discomfited as in the presence of royalty, was soon put at ease."

The delegation presented him with an address, bouquets and a large sum of money. Marcus, in replying to their formal greeting, assured them that "Our cause is a righteous one and it must triumph." They then settled down to informal discussions in the ship's sitting room. A journalist who covered this event was so impressed by the historical importance of the ceremony that he penned the following lines—"I thought of other magnificent failures. Christ at the time of his crucifixion was the most tragic failure of the ages. Socrates died a failure, so did Columbus. But the works of such men, human and divine, changed the course of the world. They were regarded as cranks, radicals and visionaries, and for them the path of glory led but to the grave. . . . I am thus inclined to think that he will ever remain the preacher and that his preachings . . . have caused his people to think, like the utterances of some of the magnificent failures who preceded him, [and that he] will some day change the course of the world."

The farewell at New Orleans had been impressive and touching. The greeting at the Canal Zone was of necessity subdued, though moving. But the welcome which awaited Marcus Mosiah Garvey in Kingston, Jamaica was so stupendous that even seasoned reporters found themselves at a loss for words to fully describe the frenzy of love and devotion which erupted over Kingston, as the largest crowds in Jamaica's history turned out to pay homage to their returning hero.

In the Canal Zone Garvey had boarded the *Santa Marta* for the final leg of his journey home. The ship was expected in Kingston in the early afternoon of Saturday December 10, 1927, but dense crowds began gathering in Kingston from early that morning. A *Daily Gleaner* reporter, in a moving account of the happenings of that day, described the "seething mass" which "crowded the thoroughfares from the United Fruit Company's pier to Liberty Hall. . . ." "Marcus Garvey's arrival in Kingston," the reporter wrote, "was perhaps the most historic event that has taken place in the metropolis of this island."

The *Santa Marta* steamed into Kingston harbour shortly after 4:00 P.M., over three hours late, but the crowds were in ebullient spirits, despite their all day vigil. "Never has any such enthusiasm been evinced," wrote the *Daily Gleaner* reporter—"To those present Garvey has been the modern Moses." Soon the figure of Marcus Garvey was recognized on the second deck and a deafening ovation went up from the assembled multitude. The reporter commented, "It was Marcus Garvey, the idol of the coloured people and his identity could not be mistaken. He readily responded to the applause that was given him and no one who saw what occurred could mistake that on board there was a person whose name all nations had to conjure with. Mr. Garvey carried under his arm a portfolio which made him appear as a Minister of State and truly it can be said that notwithstanding the number of passengers the vessel brought to this port, the humble Jamaican who came from the garden parish and rose to fame by his dynamic force . . . was the predominant figure, acclaimed and worshipped by the people of his race on account of his great idealism." The crowd could not contain its excitement, and the reporter was now at a loss for words to describe what happened next. As Marcus Garvey stepped off the ship, he wrote, "The cheering of his followers and sympathizers can better be imagined than described."

A delegation of UNIA officials extended a formal welcome. With them was Garvey's young niece, Ruth Peart, and he lifted her up into his arms. The local Garveyites had planned well. The route to Liberty Hall was festooned with banners and decorations of red, black and green. Marcus was placed in the car of Mr. Wells Elliott, a Kingston merchant. Then, preceded by detachments of Jamaican UNIA divisions and their bands, the entourage wended its way to Liberty Hall on King Street. The whole route was jammed with thousands of people. "No denser crowd has ever been witnessed in Kingston," the *Gleaner* reporter observed. At times the crowd was so thick that the car could scarcely move. At one point the people closed in on the car and expressed a desire to carry their hero the rest of the way on their shoulders. Marcus, for his part, alternated between waving his hat and stretching out both arms to shake as many hands from the crowd as he could. A large contingent of policemen lined the route, and they only added to the impressiveness of the spectacle.

Garvey's car arrived eventually at Liberty Hall, where he was to deliver an address. But the hall was packed tight and many thousands more jammed the streets outside. Getting into the hall would have been

Photo: Tony Martin

At Garveyville, Jamaica, August 20, 1981 — Byron Moore, founder, at right.

Photo: Tony Martin

Garvey's office at 2 Beaumont Crescent, West Kensington, London, photographed in 1982 — note plaque.

difficult and if even he succeeded then the thousands
outside would not have heard him. So a quick decision
was taken. He would make a short speech from the
running board of his car and would speak at a larger
venue the following night. His speech outside Liberty
Hall lasted about three minutes. He said, "My dear
friends—I can assure you it has been a great source of
satisfaction to me to return to Jamaica, the land of
my birth. The wonderful reception which you have
accorded me this afternoon has stirred my soul to the
fullest. Coming back to Jamaica, I feel deeply grati-
fied, for I know the Negroes of this island appreciate
what ever I have done for their advancement. Your
behaviour has been most exemplary and I can assure
you that as long as I live I shall do everything for
your advancement, well knowing that the organization which has been established for your uplift, will
always receive your fullest support."

Brief as this speech was, the crowd still interrupted
it with repeated bursts of applause. This part of the
day's proceedings came to an end with the playing of
the UNIA's "Universal Ethiopian Anthem" and Marcus was taken away to a well-earned night's rest.

To supplement his brief address, he gave a statement to the press that night. It was a masterful com-
position. He sought to put the local British authorities
at ease while subtly serving notice on them that he
would work to his utmost to help the poor masses of
Jamaica. The opening paragraph read, "I am glad to
be once more in Jamaica. The country seems as inviting as it ever was. To be away is to lose its touch of

nature, to return is to realize that all the world is not frigid and soulless. One can see and learn so much from the natural beauty of the island, that it is hard to imagine that in the midst of such beauty there can exist so much suffering that must appeal to human love and fellowship. To any heart this must teach the lesson of the relationship of God and man. God is good, the country is beautiful and it is man's duty to share it with his fellowman, but unfortunately it seems that one section is extremely happy whilst another is sadly poor."

The more substantial speech that Marcus had promised took place the following night at the Ward Theatre. Renewed scenes of jubilation awaited him there, as a capacity crowd quickly filled the theatre long before the scheduled hour. Hundreds were turned away and milled about outside. Prominent citizens sat on the platform and H.A.L. Simpson chaired the meeting. Marcus' remarks expanded those of his statement to the press. He would be law abiding, and he would not set out to threaten anybody's political power, but he would not be stopped from working in the interests of his suffering people. "My fore-parents, my grandparents and my mother and father," he declared, "did not suffer and die to give me an education to oppress or to slight or to discourage my people. Whatsoever education I acquired out of their sacrifice of over 300 years, I shall use for the salvation of the 400 million Negroes of the world, and the day when I forsake my people, may God Almighty say 'There shall be no more light for you.'"

Garvey's feeling for the oppressed was deep. He
continued, "When I look upon the people of this
country, their naked condition—their dirty and dis-
eased condition—do you think that I, so long as there
is a God, could keep my mouth closed and my soul
steady as a Black man, and let the foreigner sap the
wealth of this country while our people die in poverty?"

Marcus did not spare his own people either. He
reminded them that God gave them the same potential as anyone else. God, he explained, "made man,
the Lord of His creation, gave him ownership and
possession of the world, and you have been so darned
lazy that you have allowed the other fellow to run
away with the whole world and now he is bluffing
you and letting you know that the world belongs to
him and that you have no share in it."

In order to give his people confidence in self, he
included in his speech a short lesson on Black history.
He showed that Africans had led the world in civilization and he foresaw the fulfillment of the biblical
prophecy contained in the Book of Psalms that
"Princes shall come out of Egypt; Ethiopia shall
soon stretch out her hands unto God." This proved,
he said, that Africans would rise again and recapture
their ancient glory. "I have not to apologise to anybody for being black," he thundered, "because God
Almighty knew what He was doing when He made
me black." He told his audience to disregard the prejudiced historians of the twentieth century and read
what the ancient Greeks had to say. The Greek historians would prove "that when white people of

Europe were existing in continental barbarism and were cavemen, eating their own dead and sucking their own blood, over Ethiopia [the Greek word for Africa] the Gods had a progressive civilisation, because the Greeks looked upon us then as Gods. The Greeks in their mythology used to say that the Gods of Greece were gone over to Ethiopia—black men of Ethiopia." If Black people knew their glorious past, then, Marcus argued, they would be more inclined to respect themselves. All other races saw beauty in themselves, he explained, and the African must not be an exception to the rule. "I shall teach the black man to see beauty in himself," he concluded, "and be hanged to the man who says, 'It shall not be so.'"

A week later, on December 18, 1927, Marcus returned to the Ward Theatre with a long account of his work in the United States, entitled "My Advent, Work, Persecution, Indictment, Conviction, Appeal, Imprisonment and Liberation in the United States of America—the land of my friends and my enemies."

He then set out on a tour of the island, resulting in the establishment of several new UNIA branches. Meanwhile the excitement caused by his return continued. From Harlem the *Negro World* reported that "Hon. Marcus Garvey, President-General of the Universal Negro Improvement Association, now in the island of Jamaica, British West Indies, continues to be almost the exclusive topic of conversation in church and school, hut and mansion, at street corners and in the sanctuaries of the mighty in this British possession. No incident within living memory has so fired the imagination of the populace. . . ."

In the midst of this royal homecoming a few dis-
cordant voices could be heard. For not everyone in
Jamaica wished to see Marcus Garvey back. In fact,
the governor had earlier tried to get the United States
government not to deport him, so much did he fear
Garvey's presence. And the *Daily Gleaner* now came
out openly against his return. "It is with profound
regret," this paper commented, "that we view the
arrival of Marcus Garvey back in Jamaica." The
Gleaner was especially upset that some prominent
Jamaicans had joined the masses in welcoming the
hero home. "Kingston has reached such a level of
degeneracy," it moaned, "that there is no knowing
what she will do. . . . A new spirit has passed over the
lower classes which has nothing to commend it except its ignorance. . . ."

Europe, 1928

Marcus had hoped to visit both Central America and
Europe in 1928, but the Central American nations
refused him entry. He therefore left Jamaica in April
1928 for England and Europe. On his arrival in Liverpool he and his wife immediately ran into English
racism. He was denied the use of St. George's Hall
for a lecture. In London there was more of the same.
The Garveys spent a goodly portion of one day driv-
ing around to about fifty first and second class hotels.
Every single one refused to accommodate them because of their race. They finally found lodgings, to
their great surprise, at the Cecil, one of London's
most expensive hotels. Garvey figured that the Cecil
let them in only because the persons in charge knew

who he was. Even here, though, their problems were not over. White American guests objected to the Garveys' presence. In any event, the Cecil was too expensive for them to spend much time there. They moved first to a boarding house and then rented a house of their own.

On June 6, 1928 Marcus delivered a speech to the English people at the Royal Albert Hall. A disappointing two hundred persons turned up. Their numbers seemed even fewer in the vast auditorium. Marcus told them that almost ninety percent of the Black people in Britain were unemployed, due to colour prejudice.

His stay in London also enabled Marcus to strengthen his ties with a group of students known as the West African Students' Union (or WASU). WASU was led by Ladipo Solanke of Nigeria, a man who had long admired Garvey. For over ten years WASU had looked after the interests of students of African descent in Britain. Although composed mostly of British West Africans, persons from other parts of Africa, as well as the Caribbean and Afro-America also participated in its activities. Many WASU members later became influential politicians and officials in their home countries. Marcus rented a house in London's West Kensington district for WASU. This became the group's first premises of its very own. Among the persons who lived at this house was a young London University student, Johnstone Kenyatta. He is best known as Jomo Kenyatta, first president of independent Kenya.

Later in the year Marcus visited France, Belgium, Germany and the League of Nations in Geneva, Switzerland. In Paris he conferred with Africans from the French colonies. In Geneva he presented a document entitled "Renewal of Petition of the Universal Negro Improvement Association and African Communities' League to the League of Nations." The document outlined the problems facing the African race worldwide.

The Garveys left England in September for Montreal, Canada. There Marcus was arrested after making a speech commenting on the upcoming United States presidential elections. At Bermuda, their next stop, a large contingent of soldiers and police were on hand to make sure that he did not land. Marcus was scheduled to lecture in Hamilton that night and Amy Jacques Garvey, herself an excellent speaker, stood in for him. From Bermuda the Garveys proceeded to the Bahamas. This time Marcus was allowed in and he spoke in Nassau.

Sixth International Convention

One year after his triumphant return from Atlanta, Marcus was now home once more. This time around he set out to involve himself more fully in Jamaican life and politics. He began, as usual, by starting a newspaper, the *Blackman,* early in 1929. Workers now began coming to him with their grievances and he championed their cause. In May 1929 banana carriers on the docks marched to his new headquarters at Edelweis Park and asked him to represent them in negotiations with the United Fruit Company. Marcus obliged. He protested an assault on one of the workers and also the half-naked condition in which the female labourers worked. Tourists loved to take photographs of these ragged women and Garvey considered this a scandalous situation. The company threatened to adopt labour saving devices and lay off workers and the *Daily Gleaner* endorsed this suggestion. Garvey warned the editor of this paper, "the mouthpiece of special privilege and cold blooded capital in the Island of Jamaica," as he called it, to "keep his monstrous 'paws' off the situation," or the *Blackman* would "tell him where he ought to get off at. ..."

Edelweis Park meanwhile became his center of activity. He spoke there regularly. Cultural shows were also performed there. A resident UNIA choir, a Universal Jazz Hounds orchestra and plays performed by a UNIA dramatic company all became regular fare.

As usual, Marcus could not please everybody. Some disliked his stand on the local colour question. His *Blackman* newspaper offended some sections of the population in April 1929 when it bluntly blamed colour prejudice for the fact that in Kingston "we cannot find a black girl or boy in store or office," even though well-qualified ones were "refused at places filled with half illiterate brown and mulatto girls and boys affecting the attitude of superiors. ..." A month after this editorial appeared Marcus received a note from a self-styled "Jamaican Secret Society of Coloured Men." They promised to kill him by June 3, 1929, but got only as far as leaving a small snake on his doorstep. Marcus called them the "coloured Klan," after the Ku Klux Klan of the United States. He said he had some bullets waiting for them.

While all of this was going on, Marcus was working hard on plans to stir Jamaica and astound the world once more. This time he would do it through the Sixth International Convention of the Negro Peoples of the World. The convention was along the same lines as those in New York and lasted, as before, from August 1st to 31st. The opening ceremonies provided Kingston with another memorable spectacle. By 9:30 A.M., 12,000 delegates from all over the world were already assembled at Edelweis Park for early morning prayers. From there the multitude, which grew to an estimated 25,000 people, paraded for five miles through Kingston. Some ninety thousand cheering spectators jammed the route. A female UNIA official complete with military uniform and drawn sword, led the parade on a white horse. Marcus rode in an open car which was bedecked in the red, black and green of the UNIA. He wore scarlet robes and a cocked hat with red and white plumes. Various uniformed auxiliaries of the UNIA joined the parade. Some of the marchers carried a large portrait of their leader. A UNIA band provided music.

August 1st was also the anniversary of emancipation in the British West Indies and Garvey took this as the theme for his opening address. He said, "although as British Negroes we were freed in 1838, and in America as Negroes, we were freed in 1865 from chattel slavery, unfortunately we have still remained slaves; and the efforts of the Universal Negro Improvement Association are to create a second emancipation—an emancipation of the minds. . . . "

During the convention problems arose involving United States based Garveyites, some of whom had formed a rival UNIA faction in 1926 while their leader was in prison. This group now seceded from Garvey's organization and formed a rival UNIA, Incorporated, with headquarters in the United States. Garvey's faction changed its name to the Universal Negro Improvement Association and African Communities League (August 1929) of the World. Jamaica became its headquarters while Marcus remained there. The two groups did not come together again until the 1970s.

During the convention, too, the local British administration delivered the first of its long-expected blows. Extra armed police were brought into Kingston. The Argyle and Sutherland Regiment, a British force stationed in Jamaica, was also placed on alert with machine guns. Marcus did not like this at all. He said, "We understand that some of the soldiers said they were just waiting for the opportunity to shoot down Marcus Garvey and shoot down all the Negroes. . . . There is one Negro in the world, who when he dies will not die calmly except naturally—and that is Marcus Garvey . . . when anyone is getting ready to kill Marcus Garvey, he should better get ready to die himself."

The British did not kill him, but they attacked him through the courts. In the midst of the convention the chief justice fined Marcus 25 pounds for contempt of court and ordered the Kingston Liberty Hall sold. This was in connection with a suit for ar-

arrears of pay brought by George O. Marke, a former
deputy potentate. The chief justice was wrong to
force a sale, since the matter was on appeal, which
Marcus later won. The state eventually had to com-
pensate the Kingston UNIA. But by then the chief
justice had succeeded in his design of inflicting maximum damage during the convention.

Peoples' Political Party

On his arrival back from Atlanta, Marcus had said
that he had no intentions of going into local politics.
He now changed his mind. Immediately after the convention he launched his Peoples' Political Party (PPP),
the first modern political party in the British West
Indies. Garvey had his eyes on the legislative council
elections which were coming up at the end of January
1930. The PPP picked a slate of candidates, with
Marcus himself running for the St. Andrew seat. He
also prepared an election manifesto. Among its planks
were the following—self-government for Jamaica and
representation in the British parliament; protection of
native labour; a minimum wage; workmen's compen-
sation; an eight-hour working day; urban improvement; land reform and an all-Jamaica Water Board for
irrigation and other works; compulsory improvement
of urban areas by large companies which made huge
profits in those areas; promotion of local industry;
establishment of a university and polytechnic; free
secondary and night school education in each parish;
a national center for the performing arts; a law to
"impeach and imprison" unjust judges; prison reform;
the institution of legal aid; a law against buying or

otherwise unfairly obtaining votes at election time; granting Montego Bay and Port Antonio the corporate rights of cities; upgrading the Kingston Race Couse into a National Park; and a federation of the West Indies.

Marcus planned an elaborate campaign, including speeches in every parish, to explain his manifesto to the people. The thought of Marcus Garvey in the legislative council was, however, one that the local British authorities could not deal with. Marcus began his campaign with a speech to 1,500 people at Cross Roads in St. Andrew on September 9, 1929 and the authorities struck immediately. The acting deputy inspector general of police and a newspaper reporter were planted in the audience to take notes. They carefully noted the explanation of plank No. 10 of his manifesto, namely "A law to impeach and imprison such judges, who in defiance of British justice and constitutional rights will enter into illicit agreement with lawyers and other prominent businessmen to deprive other subjects of the realm of their rights . . . forcing the innocent parties to incur an additional cost of appeal, and other legal expenses. . . . "

What Garvey was complaining about in this plank was the use of the courts as a means of harassing political dissidents. He also disliked the fact that judges, who were supposed to be impartial, fraternized with lawyers and businessmen in exclusive (and often all-white) clubs.

Plank No. 10 served as a pretext for the administration to halt and disrupt Garvey's election cam-

paign. He was immediately charged with gross contempt for the king's courts and hauled before the
chief justice and two other judges. The judges took
the view that plank No. 10 implied that something
was wrong with the administration of justice in
Jamaica. As far as they were concerned, British justice in Jamaica left little or nothing to be desired
and even to suggest, in theory, a law against corrupt
judges, was a grave offence. A couple of the judges
even hinted that he should have been tried for sedi-
tion, as well as contempt. The chief justice, the same
one involved in the Marke case a few weeks earlier,
was especially offensive, and called Marcus "a hot-
headed and foolish man." The judges sentenced him
to three months in the St. Catherine District Prison
plus a fine of 100 pounds. This effectively took care
of three of the four months available to him for his
legislative council campaign.

Yet the judges could not silence Marcus by jailing
him. Another set of elections, this time for the Kingston and St. Andrew Corporation (KSAC) Council,
was due in a few weeks. Marcus now entered this
contest, campaigned from jail and handsomely won
the seat for Ward No. 3. He was released from jail
shortly before Christmas 1929 and immediately
attended three meetings of the KSAC Council. But
a majority of his colleagues then voted to have him
unseated on a technicality—he had missed three con-
secutive meetings while in jail. The newly won seat
was declared vacant and a bye-election held. Other
candidates campaigned for the seat but they later
withdrew and Marcus won the bye-election unop-

posed. The authorities had the last word for the time being when they closed down the KSAC Council altogether in September 1930. When they finally reopened it in 1931 they still could not get rid of Marcus. He remained on the Council and once the burgesses even reelected him while he was out of the country.

On his release from jail Marcus also tried to pick up the pieces of his legislative council campaign. The jail sentence had hurt him not only because it deprived him of most of his campaign time, but because it gave the judges and all his other enemies the opportunity to discredit him as "a hot-headed and foolish man." Even this did not satisfy the judges' desire to harass Garvey, though. They charged him yet again, this time with seditious libel, just a few days before the legislative council election.

Still, Marcus made the most of the short time remaining. He toured his own constituency and moved around the country speaking in support of other candidates. He attracted large crowds wherever he went. He emphasized in his speeches that he was struggling for the poor and oppressed Africans of Jamaica. He said over and over again that he was not against the white man, but as an African he could not help but put the interests of his own people first and foremost. Someone attending a Garvey speech in St. Ann reported his remarks as follows—"If he were a white man," said Garvey, "it was only natural that he would have the interests of the white people at heart; if he was a Chinaman, it was but natural that he would make all he could and send the profits to China. . . . If he was a Syrian, he would sell his cloth,

which he bought at three pence, for one shilling and
nine pence, if he could get it, and send the money to
Syria. But he . . . was a Negro, and it was therefore
nothing wrong that he should have the interest of the
Negro nearest and dearest to his heart."

Marcus lost the St. Andrew seat to the incum-
bent, G. Seymour Seymour, a white man who had
been mayor of the corporate area up to shortly before the elections. He claimed that Seymour distributed rum, sugar water and bread to Black voters.
Even before the elections he had charged *Gleaner*
editor, H. G. DeLisser, with creating the impression
that Marcus had Afro-Jamaicans in as serious a state
of unrest as during the Morant Bay Rebellion in
1865. But there was another, more important reason
for his defeat. The bulk of Garvey's followers were
the poor Black people of Jamaica and they did not
have the vote. Only the relatively well off (well under
10 per cent of the population throughout the British
West Indies) were allowed to vote in legislative council elections at that time.

Garvey's enemies had a field day after this set-
back. They attributed his defeat to the good judge-
ment of the "more thoughtful members of his race."
They called him a fraud and a cheat and one oppo-
nent referred to the UNIA as "nothing but a howling
farce." Dunbar Theophilus Wint, a Black teacher who
successfully defended his St. Ann seat against a PPP
candidate, called Garveyism "a poisonous cult." He
saw Garvey's introduction of party politics as an
attempt to fill the council with PPP members, over
whom he would then rule as a dictator.

The election defeat did not end Garvey's problems. The judges now proceeded to try the seditious libel case. Marcus, they charged, had now offended His Majesty's Government in Jamaica. The offending statement was an article written by the literary editor of the *Blackman* newspaper, criticizing the Kingston and St. Andrew Corporation Council for declaring Garvey's seat vacant. The article called the majority of councillors a bunch of vagabonds and pointed out that the government was indecent and stupid. Even though Marcus had not himself written the article, he was sentenced to six months in jail. The author of the article got three months. Marcus appealed successfully. As he had pointed out in plank No. 10, however, the judges could still make an innocent person spend large amounts of time and money proving himself innocent.

On the KSAC Council Marcus waged a lonely and largely fruitless fight for a minimum wage and an eight hour day for the council's workers. Before the dissolution of the council he put forward a motion setting forth his ideas on the relief of employment and the improvement of water, sewerage and other services. He urged the council to ask the central government to raise a loan of half a million pounds locally for these purposes. With the increase in unemployment caused by worldwide depression, he pointed out that Britain, the United States and other countries had introduced measures to help the unemployed. These included the "dole" in Britain, free meals for school children and other schemes. In Jamaica, he argued, the poor were left to fend for themselves. He suggested that Jamaica had enough money to finance his proposed scheme. Just the other day, he noted, a Jamaican had died leaving an estate worth 650,000 pounds. People that rich in other countries endowed hospitals and other worthwhile causes, he said. But not in Jamaica. This super wealthy man had contributed nothing to charitable causes. Such persons should be compelled to finance unemployment relief. If they did not, they would lose in the long run, for, Marcus warned, hungry men have no reason and the situation was already urgent. The council considered his plan too socialistic and voted it down.

Last Jamaican Years

Outside of the KSAC Council, Marcus carried on his normal round of activities. Edelweis Park continued to be a center of cultural and political attraction. In 1932 he held elocution contests in Kingston, as he had done in his youth. In June 1930 he organized a Workers and Labourers Association. The purpose of this body was not to act as a trade union itself, but to encourage workers to form unions. Garvey's two sons were also born in this period—Marcus, Jr. in 1930 and Julius in 1933. In 1931 he visited the League of Nations once more.

Meanwhile, the worldwide UNIA continued to fragment. Without Garvey's strong presence at the Harlem stronghold, UNIA branches around the world either fell into inactivity or split into rival factions. Many Garveyites joined other radical organizations, many of them very little different in their doctrines from the UNIA. Many of these new organizations continued to regard Marcus as a spiritual forerunner and a prophet.

Even with all its problems, though, the UNIA was much too strong an organization to collapse suddenly and disappear. It remained an important force in the United States and some other places for many years. And the *Negro World* remained faithful to Marcus until it ceased publication in 1933. Marcus continued to send in his front page editorials from Jamaica. He also kept up his Jamaican publications. The *Blackman* ceased publication in 1931 and was followed by the *New Jamaican*, an evening paper, from 1932 to 1933. The *Black Man* magazine followed the *New Jamaican* in December 1933.

In 1934 the Seventh International Convention of the Negro Peoples of the World was held in Kingston. Delegates came up with a five year plan to try and regain the former splendour of the UNIA. They also sanctioned a move by Marcus to London. Here, in a major world capital, it seemed that he might be in a better position to maintain contact with his scattered organization. Here, too, Marcus might find some relief from the legal and financial harassments which plagued him in Jamaica. For the British often tended to be much more despotic in their colonies than they dared to be at home. As for financial problems, Marcus in December 1934 lost Edelweis Park to sale by the mortgagor. He left Jamaica for the last time in 1935.

Rastafarians

The Rastafarian movement had its beginnings in Jamaica in the early 1930s, while Marcus was active in the island. Many of the original Rastafarians were also Garveyites. The movement was not a single, unified body, but rather a loose association of individuals and groups holding similar, but not necessarily identical beliefs. They preached a Black nationalist philosophy of race pride, the need for a strong African nation and other ideas reminiscent of Garveyism. Many Rastafarians looked forward to repatriation to Africa, even as Marcus had earlier tried to move his headquarters to Liberia. The best-known aspect of the Rastafarian belief is its interest in Ethiopia as the African homeland and the belief by some sections of the movement in the late Emperor Haile Selassie I of Ethiopia as God.

One does not have to look far in the UNIA to see where early Rastafarians may have discovered Ethiopia. Marcus frequently used the word in its ancient sense, meaning Africa in general. (The word was actually coined by the ancient Greeks, for whom it signified "Land of the Burnt Faces," or place where the Black people lived). This is why the UNIA's anthem was the "Universal Ethiopian Anthem." In his speeches Marcus often quoted the famous biblical prediction from the 68th Psalm, that "Princes shall come out of Egypt; Ethiopia shall soon stretch out her hands unto God."

Before becoming emperor, Haile Selassie had long shown an interest in Garveyism and in the Africans of the West. In 1922, while he was prince regent, he sent a message to the UNIA in New York inviting Africans from the West to come and help build Ethiopia. In 1930 several Garveyites heeded that call, led by Barbados-born Arnold J. Ford. Ford had for years been musical director of the UNIA and had composed the Universal Ethiopian Anthem in 1919.

It was in 1930, too, that Ethiopia really stirred the imaginations of African peoples like never before. For November that year saw the coronation of Haile Selassie I, King of Kings, Lord of Lords and Conquering Lion of the Tribe of Judah. The coronation was a lavish spectacle and was widely reported by the media, both Black and non-Black. In Jamaica, Garvey's *Blackman* newspaper greeted the event with front page portraits of Selassie and Garvey. Marcus sent a telegram of congratulations to Haile Selassie and the *Blackman* told Jamaicans that Ras Tafari "is ready and willing to extend the hand of invitation to any Negro who desires to settle in his kingdom."

As the small Rastafarian movement developed, its members remained close to the UNIA and sometimes were even allowed to use a little space in the Kingston UNIA office. In 1934 Rastafarians asked Garvey's permission to sell portraits of Haile Selassie at the UNIA's international convention. Garvey allowed them to sell the photographs, though not from his platform, as some had requested. Still, Garvey seems to have disapproved of the activities of at least some of these early Rastafarians, for he said so during one of his 1934 convention speeches. More differences of opinion between Garvey and some Rasta-

farians were to come over the Italian-Ethiopian War
(see Chapter 11). None of these differences was serious enough to dislodge Marcus from the position of
reverence in which Rastafarians (and, indeed, other
UNIA offshoot groups) have held him over the years.

11

Last London Years: 1935-1940

London

Marcus Garvey left Jamaica in April 1935. He never set foot in his native island again. In London he made what was to be his final effort at a comeback on the world scene. He set himself up in modest quarters and soon resumed the only activity that he knew. He contacted the surviving UNIA units around the world, encouraging the strengthening of existing branches and the formation of new ones. He appealed for money for his programs and units from the United States, South Africa, the West Indies and elsewhere responded, as in the old days. He spoke to interracial audiences, especially at Speakers' Corner, Hyde Park, where he became a regular attraction. He also contacted London-based organizations, such as the International African Service Bureau (IASB), led by George Padmore of Trinidad. He made a small financial contribution to the IASB.

Marcus could not operate without a publication of some kind and so he continued in London to bring out his *Black Man* magazine. It sometimes appeared at irregular intervals due to insufficient funds and staff, but Marcus would not let it die. Though not as powerful as the *Negro World* in its heyday, the *Black Man* nevertheless got around quite well. It was read widely around the world.

In order to train a new cadre of leaders to carry on the work of the UNIA, Marcus established the School of African Philosophy. The school ran correspondence courses through which Marcus passed on the knowledge and experience of a lifetime of political work. Later, in Canada, he held resident courses where he administered the lessons in person. One of the two surviving graduates of the school in 1980 was Chicago-based Hon. Charles L. James, president general of the UNIA.

Italo-Ethiopian War

In October 1935, a few months after Garvey's arrival in London, the Italian fascist dictator, Benito Mussolini, sent an invading army into Ethiopia. Haile Selassie's forces were sadly lacking in modern weapons and were no match for the Italians with their warplanes and poison gas.

African peoples all over the world rallied to the defence of Ethiopia. It is generally agreed that no event to that time, save the rise of the UNIA, caused such a worldwide mobilization of African peoples. Pro-Ethiopian activity was widespread in the Caribbean. Prayer meetings were held in Barbados. In

Trinidad dockworkers refused to handle Italian ships and local Yorubas held ceremonies on Ethiopia's behalf. In November 1935 2,500 Trinidadians attended an open-air service marking the fifth anniversary of Haile Selassie's coronation. From British Guiana (Guyana), Trinidad, St. Lucia and Jamaica young men bombarded the British authorities wtih requests for permission to volunteer to fight for Ethiopia. A Jamaican UNIA petition contained 1,400 signatures from would-be volunteers. Mrs. Amy Jacques Garvey, who did not join her husband in England until 1937, addressed a pro-Ethiopia rally at Kingston's Liberty Hall. Riots in St. Vincent were partly inflamed by the Italian invasion.

In Afro-America, too, a large number of pro-Ethiopia organizations sprang up. Many were led by Garveyites and former Garveyites. In England, Trinidad-born C.L.R. James formed the International African Friends of Abyssinia (Ethiopia).

Garvey attacked Mussolini and the Italians bitterly in issue after issue of the *Black Man*. He lent all his support to the Ethiopians. He was, however, critical of Haile Selassie. He thought that Selassie was partly to blame for keeping Ethiopia militarily and socially weak. He also felt that Selassie should have remained in Ethiopia to rally his troops, rather than fleeing to England. He expressed himself this way—"No one desires to be unfair to Haile Selassie. The only sad thing is that he has been unfair to himself . . . whilst other nations and rulers are building up armaments of the most destructive kind, as the only means of securing peace and protection, he relied on the peculiar

policy of leaving everything to the Almighty Wisdom
of the Universal Creator, Who in all history, has never
yet taken political sides between two rival human
political forces and powers. . . . When Ethiopia again
stretches forth her hand to God, it will have to be
a hand of progress."

Coming in the midst of all the widespread support
for the Ethiopians, Garvey's criticisms seemed strange
and confusing to many. Some of his former followers
in Jamaica, the United States and elsewhere now attacked him on this score. To them it must have
seemed as though Garvey was withdrawing support
from the Ethiopian cause, though such was not in
fact the case.

Bring Back Garvey

Even after ten years of absence from the United States
and despite the various splits in the UNIA there, Marcus still commanded a respectable following among
Afro-Americans. They still consulted him on a regular
basis and he retained enough influence to arbitrate
some of their UNIA-related disputes from England.
They, in turn, never gave up their efforts to get him
readmitted into the United States. They were convinced that if Marcus could only find a way back, his
powerful personality would once again unite the
UNIA, attract new members and generally raise the
race out of the terrible suffering of the 1930s depression. They therefore plied politicians, from the president of the United States on down, with letters,
telegrams and petitions requesting a lifting of the ban
on their leader. They sought help from whoever,

Black or white, seemed to offer a sympathetic ear. They were still trying when Marcus died in 1940.

Canada and the West Indies

Since he could not get into the United States, Marcus visited Canada in 1936, 1937 and 1938. Here he gave speeches in such places as Nova Scotia, Toronto and Windsor, Ontario, just across the U.S. border from Detroit. Many United States Garveyites crossed the border to hear him on these occasions. Some stayed to attend the residential courses for his School of African Philosophy. In August 1938 he held the Eighth and last International Convention of the Negro Peoples of the World, in Toronto.

It was from Halifax, Nova Scotia, that Marcus sailed on his final West Indian tour in 1937. He visited St. Kitts, Nevis, Antigua, Montserrat, Dominica, St. Lucia, St. Vincent, Grenada, Barbados, Trinidad and British Guiana (Guyana). His ship did not stop at Jamaica. He spoke to large and enthusiastic crowds everywhere for, whatever his personal fortunes, the name Garvey was still magic. He was dined and entertained by local committees, often of prominent citizens, many of whom had been UNIA members or sympathizers.

Even at this late stage of his life, Marcus in the West Indies still seemed a threat to the British officials. As already seen in Chapter 6, they considered preventing him from landing in Trinidad, but agreed to allow him in after Deputy Mayor, Captain A. A. Cipriani, came to his assistance. Even so, however, Marcus was still forbidden from making any political speeches, or referring to the recent workers' riots in Trinidad, or holding any outdoor meetings. Back in England, he summed up his trip in verse—

> My trip to the West Indies has proven a boon,
> I hope to come this way again soon. . . .

Trinidad was not the only Caribbean island experiencing labour unrest in the late 1930s. Workers in other islands, including Jamaica, were also fighting for a square deal and a more democratic society. Both in Trinidad in 1937 and in Jamaica in 1938, rumours spread that Garvey would appear on the scene. Many of the activists involved were present or former Garveyites. Among them was St. William Grant of Jamaica, former head of the UNIA "Tiger" division in New York. Grant returned home in 1934 for the Seventh International Convention of the Negro Peoples of the World and decided to stay. He quickly became a popular figure for his streetcorner meetings on Garveyism. Sometimes these meetings attracted crowds of several thousand people. Grant played a prominent role in the turmoil of 1938 and was jailed together with Alexander Bustamante, the major new leader to emerge at that time. Marcus supported these workers' struggles in the *Black Man* magazine. In 1938 he submitted a memorandum to the West India Royal Commission which was investigating the disturbances. Here he traced the history of discriminations facing Afro-Jamaicans since emancipation. This, he explained, was the real cause of the riots of 1938.

The End

In January 1940 Marcus suffered a stroke that left him paralysed on the right side and unable to speak. This was not his first illness in England. Since leaving Jamaica he had had two bouts of pneumonia. He was also a chronic sufferer from asthma. Under the care of his doctor and small staff he improved quickly and was soon able to attend to correspondence, speak clearly and go for rides in Hyde Park, which he loved so much. He still could not walk, however. His doctor advised complete rest but work was all that Marcus knew and so he continued to tax his weakened body. In May a Black reporter in London maliciously sent out a story saying that Marcus had died. Obituaries appeared in the media all over the world. Some, from former enemies such as the Black communist, Cyril Briggs, were hostile and abusive. Clippings of these obituaries began pouring into his office. Two days of such macabre correspondence was all that Marcus could take in his weakened state and he suffered another stroke. He died on June 10, 1940. He was only fifty-two, not a very old man. But he had worn himself out in a lifetime of struggle in pursuit of a noble ideal.

12

Marcus Garvey, Hero

Underground Hero

In a speech to his Sixth International Convention of the Negro Peoples of the World in Kingston in 1929, Marcus jokingly said—"You have heard of Johnnie Walker. Well, he had his adversities but he is still going strong and I intend with your assistance and God's grace to continue." There was much laughter and applause from the delegates, and then Marcus continued—"If when the convention ends and you return to your homes in the several parts of the world you hear that I am dead, do not believe I am dead entirely but that I have just started to live."

Some Garveyites may have taken the chief (as many called him), literally, for a goodly number refused to believe when they heard the news of June 1940. S.U. Smith, a leader of the UNIA Harmony division in Jamaica, was moved to ask, "What

is wrong? Was he immortal? Was he not human and
subjected to sickness and death like the rest of us?"
A Jamaican Garveyite magazine published a photo-
graph of the corpse, in order to reassure the public.
Still, some Garveyites, especially in Jamaica, simply
refused to believe that their leader had been taken
from them. As late as 1964, when Garvey's body was
brought back home to Jamaica, controversy raged
once more, as to whether the man was really dead.
Some argued that the public was being fooled and
that the coffin contained a log or some other substitute for the body.

For those who believed that Garvey was dead,
there were two very different reactions to the news of
June 1940. In official circles everything was done to
wipe out the record of Garvey's phenomenal career.
A whole generation of schoolchildren grew up in the
West Indies, Afro-America and Africa who never saw
the name of Marcus Garvey mentioned in their history books. The man who had led the largest international political movement among Africans in history,
disappeared, as it were, from the pages of history.
Where he was mentioned, it was usually in a very few
sentences suggesting that he was probably a crook
and a fool.

In many Black communities, though, and especially among the poor and oppressed, Garvey's name
continued to live. Even while he was alive many of
his followers had looked upon him almost as a religious leader, and now that he was dead he quickly
became a hero, a prophet and a legend to many who

remembered him. Both the pro-Garvey and the break-away UNIA factions tried their best to keep his name alive, although their numbers dwindled as the years progressed.

Some of the other organizations started by former Garveyites attracted large followings and they, too, projected Garvey as a hero and prophet. One of these was the Nation of Islam (popularly known as "Black Muslims"). The Nation was started in the early 1930s by Elijah Muhammad, a former UNIA member from Detroit, Michigan, in the U.S.A. The Nation of Islam hailed Garvey as a forerunner of Elijah Muhammad, who adopted Garvey's famous slogan of "Up! You mighty race, you can accomplish what you will." The Nation of Islam, like the UNIA, preached race first and self-reliance and sought a separate Black nation. By the early 1960s it had become quite possibly the most powerful Afro-American organization. Its members at this time included heavyweight boxing champion, Muhammad Ali and Malcolm X, one of the most popular Afro-American leaders of the time.

Another organization which helped keep Garvey's name alive during the dreary years of official neglect was the Universal African Nationalist Movement, headquartered in New York. By the early 1950s it boasted thousands of members in Afro-America, St. Lucia, Trinidad, Panama, Honduras and elsewhere. Also based in New York around this time was the African Nationalist Pioneer Movement led by Carlos Cooks, whose father had been a UNIA leader in the Dominican Republic. The Rastafarians of Jamaica also played an important role in saving Garvey from total oblivion during these years.

In London, too, various organizations among the small but growing Black community honoured Garvey from time to time. At Speakers' Corner in Hyde Park in the 1940s and 1950s one could frequently hear Black orators praising Garvey's name.

The New York-based groups were responsible for the introduction of "Garvey Day" celebrations on August 17 of each year, Garvey's birthday. These celebrations are now observed in many cities across the United States and have spread to London, Trinidad and other places. In some cities as many as four, five or more organizations now hold separate "Garvey Day" celebrations on or around August 17 each year. Celebrations take many forms—commemorative meetings, lectures, fairs, beauty shows and so on.

Shortly after Garvey's death several publications appeared in the effort to keep his name alive in the face of official silence. All of these efforts had relatively small circulations. They could not force Garvey's memory onto the public at large, but they ensured that the man and his work would not fade away. In 1940 Len S. Nembhard, a Jamaican newspaperman, published the first book-length biography of Garvey, which he called the *Trials and Triumphs of Marcus Garvey*. In Jamaica, too, Z. Monroe Scarlett, a Garveyite for all his adult life, in 1941 published the weekly *National Negro Voice*. This publication was one of the first to call for erection of a statue in memory of Garvey. In the 1940s and afterwards, the

African, a Harlem magazine, circulated among Garveyites in many countries. It later changed its name
to *African Opinion.*

International Acclaim

The community groups, publications and individuals
who stubbornly held on to Garvey's memory during
the 1940s, 1950s and 1960s never did manage to
break through the wall of neglect imposed by official
circles and the mass media. However, by the late
1950s their efforts began to receive help from influential circles.

On November 4, 1956 the Kingston and St. Andrew Corporation Council unveiled a bust of Marcus
Mosiah Garvey in George VI Park, formerly Kingston
Race Course (and now National Heroes Park, a name
suggested in part by Garvey in his 1929 manifesto).
Several persons had called for such an honour since
Z. Monroe Scarlett and the *National Negro Voice*
raised the question fifteen years earlier. A large
number of celebrities were on hand for the occasion,
including UNIA officials from the United States,
Jamaican politicians, the British governor and Garvey's
widow, Amy Jacques Garvey. Over a quarter of a
century earlier members of the same KSAC Council
had tried their best to keep Garvey out of that body.
At that time the British governor and judges had been
among Garvey's tormentors. But time, death and
public sentiment had conspired to bring them together, twenty-five and more years later, to do honour
to the fallen warrior.

The very next year, 1957, Garvey received another major boost. In that year the British West African colony of the Gold Coast became the independent nation of Ghana. It was the first African or Caribbean British colony to regain its independence, apart from the Sudan. First president of the new nation was Kwame Nkrumah, a staunch admirer of Garvey and a man who had attended UNIA meetings in Harlem during his student days in the United States. Nkrumah was always ready to express his appreciation for the teachings of Marcus Garvey. He named Ghana's new shipping company the Black Star Line, after Garvey's line.

When in 1960 Nigeria followed Ghana into independence, the first governor general, Nnamdi Azikiwe, was another admirer of Garvey. Azikiwe, like Nkrumah, has testified in his autobiography to the influence which Garvey had on his political development. Among the proud guests at the inaugural of Governor General Azikiwe in November 1960 was Amy Jacques Garvey. From Nigeria Mrs. Garvey travelled to Ghana as a guest of President Nkrumah's government. Her joy was complete when she saw the president confer on Emperor Haile Selassie I of Ethiopia, "the Exalted Order of the Star of Africa—the black star."

Two years before visiting Africa, Amy Jacques Garvey had finished a biography of her husband, which she entitled *Garvey and Garveyism*. The powers that be still were not ready for a sympathetic look at the man's life and no publisher would touch it. Mrs.

Garvey was determined to play her part in the revival of interest in her husband and so in 1963 she published the book herself with borrowed money. She then mailed copies at her own expense to libraries around the world. In the early 1960s the UNIA in the United States also began publishing a weekly newspaper, *Garvey's Voice,* which carried news of the organization and reprints of Garvey's speeches.

It was clear by this time that a Garvey revival was slowly gathering steam. The movement took a tremendous leap forward in 1964, two years after Jamaica became independent, when the government agreed to bring Garvey's remains back home. On November 9, 1964 over seventy people attended a memorial service for the UNIA leader, organized by the Jamaican high commission in London. On the next day, November 10, Garvey's remains were flown back to Jamaica.

The body was received amidst much pomp and ceremony. It remained at the airport under a police guard until the following day, when it was transported by launch across the harbour to Victoria Market Pier. From here it was carried up King Street to the Holy Trinity Cathedral. There the body lay in state, guarded by soldiers, until the funeral service. Garvey's last journey was a short one, from the cathedral to George VI Park, where the remains were reinterred. At the head of the funeral procession were Amy Jacques Garvey and her two sons.

Among the guests for this occasion were delegates from thirty-two countries attending a Commonwealth Parliamentary Association conference in Jamaica. The leader of the Uganda delegation to this conference, Godfrey Binaisa, recalled reading Garvey's *Black Man* magazine as a youth, even though it was banned in Uganda. Binaisa later had a brief spell as president of his country.

After bringing Garvey's remains back home, the Jamaican government followed up by proclaiming him the country's first National Hero. Many official honours followed in the land of his birth. A highway and a school were named after him. In 1965 a Marcus Garvey Scholarship for Boys was established. In 1969, Human Rights Year, the government presented a Marcus Garvey peace award of 5,000 pounds to Coretta Scott King, on behalf of her murdered husband, Martin Luther King, Jr. In 1971 Garvey's face appeared on a Jamaican ten cent stamp and on the fifty cent note (later replaced by a fifty cent coin, which also bears his portrait). Garvey's hometown of St. Ann's Bay was not forgotten in all this. Here, a large statue was erected outside of the town's public library. Since 1964 it has also become standard practice for visiting dignitaries to lay a wreath at the Garvey shrine in Kingston. President Sékou Touré of Guinea laid a wreath at the shrine in 1979.

The official presentation of the insignia of the Order of National Hero, Jamaica's highest honour, was made to Amy Jacques Garvey on her husband's behalf in November 1971. The citation read as follows—"For services to Jamaica of the Most Distinguished Nature: The Rt. Excellent Marcus Garvey. Of paramount importance to the Rt. Excellent Marcus Garvey was the need for the Black Peoples of Jamaica, the Caribbean, North America, Africa and other parts of the world to recognize the dignity of their race. He dedicated his life to this cause and to the general upliftment of persons of African descent. In bestowing on him the title of 'National Hero', Jamaica pays him the nation's highest tribute."

One month later Mrs. Garvey was honoured in her own right with a Musgrave Gold Medal, awarded by the Institute of Jamaica. She became the second woman and the tenth person to achieve this honour since its inception in 1888. The Musgrave citation praised her "dedicated and distinguished contribution to the history of the people of African descent, and particularly her erudite dissertations on the philosophy of Garveyism. . . ."

While the Jamaican government and people were paying homage to Marcus Garvey and African leaders were praising his efforts, events in the United States were also pushing Marcus into the limelight once again. From the early 1950s Afro-Americans had stepped up their Civil Rights struggle for equality and an end to segregation. In the early 1960s the younger, more militant activists began to stress Black pride, Black history, the need for Black people to control their own destinies and the link with their African roots. Natural "Afro" hairstyles became popular, dashikis and African jewelry came into vogue and slogans such as "Black is beautiful" and "Black Power" were heard everywhere. As they delved into their history, this young generation of the 1960s discovered that long before they were born, there had lived in Afro-America a man who said the same things they were saying, and with phenomenal success. It was not long before the 1960s generation embraced Marcus Garvey as a major hero. His red, black and green became the colours of this new Black revolution and by the 1970s, several streets, parks, community centers, building complexes and the like had been named after him in Black communities throughout the United States.

In November 1972 in Brooklyn, New York, Jamaica's representative to the United Nations and the country's consul general in New York joined the city's mayor, John V. Lindsay, in groundbreaking ceremonies for Marcus Garvey Park Village, a U.S. $200,000,000 urban construction and rehabilitation project. The name had been voted on by residents of the area. Mayor Lindsay said on that occasion that Garvey was "the best known Jamaican to Americans," and one who would "always be remembered not only by Blacks, but by progressive thinking people for the principles of racial justice which he so sternly advocated." In 1979 similar groundbreaking ceremonies took place in Roxbury, a Black section of Boston, for Marcus Garvey Gardens, a $7,000,000 housing development.

Recognition kept coming in from other places as well. In 1969 the Federal Republic of Cameroon in West Africa issued a commemorative stamp bearing a portrait of Garvey. In 1972 in London a plaque was unveiled at 2 Beaumont Crescent, West Kensington, his offices during the last London years.

A growing number of books and other publications also helped swell the Garvey revival. Whereas in

1963 no North American or European publisher would touch Mrs. Garvey's *Garvey and Garveyism,* by the late 1960s some of these publishers were convinced that the time had come to cash in on the growing Black consciousness. By the end of the decade three major publishers had reprinted the two volume *Philosophy and Opinions of Marcus Garvey, or, Africa for the Africans,* first published by Mrs. Garvey in the 1920s. This book is a collection of Garvey's speeches and writings. The original editions were published privately and for years no publisher would reprint them. Now, all of a sudden, there were three competing editions in print. In the 1970s Black historians finally took up the challenge to present Garvey's life in a truthful and sympathetic light. For years Black students and scholars had criticized the flippant attitude to Garvey displayed by many white authors, and some Black ones too. In the 1970s scholars produced the first serious works in over thirty years, to challenge the view of Garvey as a buffoon and a crook.

After the years of official neglect, it seems that this time around Garvey is working his way back to stay. Several international gatherings were among those honouring him in the 1970s. In 1973 the African Studies Association of the West Indies organized an International Seminar on Marcus Garvey at the University of the West Indies at Mona, Jamaica. Scholars from the West Indies, the United States, Africa and Europe reported on their researches into various aspects of Garvey's life. Among those addressing the audience were Amy Jacques Garvey and Marcus Garvey, Jr. In August 1978 the UNIA, then headquartered in Philadelphia, U.S.A., brought an international gathering of several hundred people to Kingston for a conference celebrating their leader's ninety-first birthday. The organization also called for an approach to be made to United States President, Jimmy Carter, with a view to overturning Garvey's mail fraud conviction of 1923. In 1979 the United Nations Special Committee Against Apartheid held a week long conference in Kingston in honour of Marcus Garvey and five other West Indians who had contributed to the struggle against apartheid in racist South Africa. (The other five honorees were Henry Sylvester Williams and George Padmore of Trinidad; Dantes Bellegarde of Haiti; Frantz Fanon of Martinique; and José Martí of Cuba). One year later, in 1980, the Organization of American States unveiled a bronze bust of Garvey in its Hall of Heroes in Washington, D.C.

At the level of popular culture Garvey has also come into his own, thanks especially to Jamaican reggae music. He is a favourite theme for reggae singers and, by the beginning of the 1980s, was beginning to make this way into Trinidadian calypsoes and poems as well.

Garvey foresaw that future generations would have to reckon with his message. He loved the famous line from an old poem, that "Truth crushed to earth shall rise again." In the midst of the persecutions that followed him throughout his life he always found solace in this knowledge. In 1925, after being sentenced to five years in Atlanta penitentiary he wrote, in prophetic vein—"If I die in Atlanta my work shall then only begin, but I shall live, in the physical or spiritual to see the day of Africa's glory. When I am dead wrap the mantle of the Red, Black and Green around me, for in the new life I shall rise with God's grace and blessing to lead the millions up the heights of triumph with the colors that you well know. Look for me in the whirlwind or the storm, look for me all around you, for, with God's grace, I shall come and bring with me countless millions of black slaves who have died in America and the West Indies and the millions in Africa to aid you in the fight for Liberty, Freedom and Life."

13

Conclusion

Garvey's Black Star Line failed in the end; he did not succeed in moving his headquarters to Africa; he was deported from the United States; and for all the millions of dollars that passed through his hands he did not die a rich man. Yet, in the perspective of history, he was a phenomenal success. He rallied the whole African world in its hour of most desperate need. He built the largest mass movement of its kind. And his influence, in his own time and afterwards, has been profound.

Several factors can help explain Garvey's tremendous impact—

1) *The time was right.* He appeared on the scene when the need was greatest. Africa was in the last throes of European conquest and the Black world was reeling from the near total annihilation of its independence. The World War I period was also a good

161

time for Garvey to strike, because the conflict distracted the powerful colonialist powers long enough for oppressed peoples everywhere to agitate for freedom. In Afro-America the war helped in another respect—many Afro-Americans obtained employment in the war industries and for the first time in their history Afro-Americans possessed the kind of money necessary to finance a movement as ambitious as Garvey's. West Indian immigrants in Latin America shared to some extent in this new found prosperity.

2) *Garvey's personal attributes.* The time was ripe for Garvey, but the time alone cannot explain his success. For scores of other leaders tried to do what he did at the same time. None succeeded like Garvey. Garvey alone was able to seize the time so overwhelmingly. He knew his people. He taught and inspired them, and he earned the right to criticize them. Long before he burst upon the world scene, he was already imbued with a powerful sense of mission. This gave his life a singleness of purpose that allowed him to keep bouncing back after the most punishing setbacks. For those who heard him, his oratorical skill exercised a spellbinding influence. Yet many followed him who never saw him. For them his writings, especially his *Negro World* editorials, exercised the same fascination, even when they received the message second hand and by word of mouth from others who had read the paper.

3) *His practical achievements.* Garvey demonstrated that he could build viable institutions and this at-

tracted many followers. The *Negro World,* the Negro Factories Corporation and the Black Star Line were among the most striking. The effect of the Black Star Line especially, on attracting members to the UNIA, can hardly be imagined. The UNIA itself, as an umbrella for all these subsidiaries, was a massive and successful exercise in institution building.

4) *The spiritual dimension.* Many Garveyites related to Garveyism practically as to a religion, for Garvey was able to lift them out of their degradation and despair and give them hope. He provided a goal to believe in—a "free and redeemed Africa," as he put it, and a world of Black men and women proudly and fiercely equal to the rest of humankind. His ideology of race first, self-reliance and nationhood provided a self-respect that millions of his followers were in danger of losing after centuries of slavery and subjugation, reinforced by the European scramble for Africa. S. A. Haynes of Belize and later the United States, once put it this way—"Garvey sold the Negro to himself."

It took the power of government to get Garvey out of the United States and slowly weaken the UNIA. If he had succeeded in establishing himself in Liberia this problem may have been avoided, but such was not to be. Yet, no power could prevent the influence which he has continued to exert on organizations and individuals since his death. As he himself was so fond of saying, "Truth crushed to earth shall rise again."

Photo: Tony Martin

Hon. Charles L. James, President-General, UNIA — Brooklyn, New York, January 18, 1981

Photo: Tony Martin

The Garvey celebration is over, but someone turned on the sound system — Ward Theatre, Kingston, Jamaica, August 21, 1981

Some Suggestions For Further Reading

Clarke, John Henrik, ed. *Marcus Garvey and the Vision of Africa*. New York: Random House, 1974.

Garvey, Amy Jacques. *Garvey and Garveyism*. New York: Collier Books, 1970.

———, ed. *Philosophy and Opinions of Marcus Garvey, or, Africa for the Africans*. Dover, Mass.: The Majority Press, 1986 (first pub. 1923,1925).

Martin, Tony. *Literary Garveyism: Garvey, Black Arts and The Harlem Renaissance*. Dover, Mass.: The Majority Press, 1983.

———. *The Pan-African Connection*. Dover, Mass.: The Majority Press, 1984.

———. *Race First: The Ideological and Organizational Struggles of Marcus Garvey and the Universal Negro Improvement Association*. Dover, Mass.: The Majority Press, 1986 (first pub. 1976)

Nembhard, Lenford Sylvester. *Trials and Triumphs of Marcus Garvey*. Millwood, N.Y.: Kraus Reprint Co., 1978.

Garvey memorial, St. Ann's Bay, Jamaica.

Photo: *Tony Martin*

Index

Adam, Jean Joseph, 80
Aduwa, Battle of, 29
Africa, 2, 7, 8, 29, 32, 52, 53, 54, 57, 61, 65, 67, 76, 103, 107, 125, 138, 153, 157, 158, 160, 163; scramble for, 28–29; all Black people citizens of, 63; and Bible, 77; Garveyism in, 85–95; Garvey's proposed tour of, 87; led world in civilization, 122
African, The, 152
African Blood Brotherhood, 103
African Methodist Episcopal (AME) Church, 40, 43, 81
African Motor Corps, 60
African National Congress, 87, 113
African Nationalist Pioneer Movement, 75, 150

African Opinion, 152
African Orthodox Church, 52, 78, 93
African Studies Association of the West Indies, 158
Africa Times and Orient Review, 19–22
Afro-America, 2; conditions in, 29–30; internal emigration, 30; UNIA in, 96–98; and Italo-Ethiopian War, 143
Ali, Dusé Mohamed, 20, 150
Alves, A. Bain, 31
Angola, 95
Antigua, 37, 52, 145; UNIA in, 78
Anti-slavery and Aborigines Protection Society, 22
Antonio Maceo, S.S., 57
Argyle and Sutherland Regiment, 129

167

Aruba, 80
Ashwood, Amy. *See* Amy Ashwood Garvey
Atlanta penitentiary, 112, 159
Austria, 19
Australia, 86, 99
Azikiwe, Nnamdi, 90-92, 153

Bagnall, Rev. Robert W., 109
Bahamas, 12, 56, 126
Balkis, 77
Barbados, 3, 6, 7, 57, 70, 81, 93, 139, 142, 145; emigration from, to Liberia, 7; UNIA in, 75-76
Barclay, Arthur, 7
Barclay, Edwin, 8
Barnett, Ida Wells, 41
Barrow, Bishop Reginald, 75
Basutoland. *See* Lesotho
Bechuanaland. *See* Botswana
Beckles, John, 75, 76
Beecher, J. Coleman, 31
Belgian Congo. *See* Zaire
Belgium, 125
Belize, 54; 1919 unrest, 59; UNIA in, 77-78
Bellegarde, Dantes, 159
Benjamin, P.A., 11
Berlin Conference, 28
Bermuda, 81; prohibits Garvey from landing, 81, 126
Bible, 45, 77
Binaisa, Godfrey, 93, 155
Birkbeck College, 19
Black Cross Navigation and Trading Co., 112

Black Cross Nurses, in New York, 60; in St. Thomas, 76; in Belize, 77
Black history, 63, 122
Blackman (newspaper), 126, 127, 135, 137, 139
Black Man (magazine), 93, 137, 142, 146, 155
Black Muslims. *See* Nation of Islam
Black nationalism, 106, 138
Black Power, 156
Black Star Line, 55-58, 61, 74, 79, 94, 96, 104, 107, 110, 111, 114, 161, 163; Lagos office, 90
Black Star Line (of Ghana), 153
Black Star Line band, 61
Blyden, Edward Wilmot, 7, 20, 77
Bogle, Paul, 13, 14
Booker T. Washington, S.S., 112
Book of Psalms, 122
Botswana, 88
Brazil, 83
Briggs, Cyril, 147
British Guiana. *See* Guyana
British Guiana Labour Union, 74
British Honduras. *See* Belize
British West Indian Review, 101
British West Indies Regiment, 58-59, 77
Bruce, John Edward, 41

Burrows, Mr., 10
Bustamante, Alexander, 146
Butler, Tubal Uriah Buzz, 73

Cadet, Eliezer, 80
Caeser, Julius, 22
Calypsoes, 159
Cambridge University, 3
Cameroon, 157
Canada, 48, 60, 66, 109, 114, 126, 142; UNIA convention in, 64; UNIA in, 98; Garvey visits in 1936, 1937 and 1938, 145
Candace, 77
Cape Verde Islands, 95
Carter, President Jimmy, 159
Casimir, J.R. Ralph, 78-79
Castro, Fidel, 71
Cecil, The, 124-25
Chatham, Lord, 12, 34
Chen, Eugene, 64
Chile, 16
China, 2, 64, 133
Cipriani, Capt. A.A., 72, 73, 145
Crichlow, Hubert, 74
Christ, Jesus, 116
Christian Science Monitor, The, 37
Cockburn, Capt. Joshua, 56, 111
Codrington College, 3, 7
Colombia, 6, 83
Colón Federal Labour Union, 17
Colonial Office, 19

Columbus, Christopher, 116
Commonwealth Parliamentary Association, 154
Communist International, 101
Communist Party of the U.S.A., 104
Communists, 102-04
Cooks, Carlos, 75, 150
Coolidge, President Calvin, 113
Costa Rica, 7, 15, 16, 74, 101; West Indian emigration to, 6; UNIA in, 82-83
Cox, S.A.G., 14
Cuba, 1, 56, 57, 74, 97, 112, 159; emigration to Zaire, 8; UNIA in, 69-71, 82

Dahomey, 94, 95
Daily Gleaner, 117, 118, 124, 127, 134
DeBourg, John Sydney, 72
Declaration of Rights of the Negro Peoples of the World, 62
De Lisser, H. G., 134
De Valera, Eamon, 64
Dixon, Alexander, 14
Dominica, 57, 145; UNIA in, 78-79
Dominican Republic, 57, 150; UNIA in, 74
DuBois, W.E.B., 90, 106; on Garvey's physical features, 109
Dunbar, Paul Laurence, 33

Duncan, Samuel Augustus, 105
Dutch Guiana. *See* Suriname

East Queen St. Baptist Church Hall, 30
Ecuador, 6, 16, 83
Edelweis Park, 126, 127, 128, 136; sold by mortgagor, 137
Edinburgh University, 3
Egypt, 20, 52, 122, 138
Elizabeth I, Queen, 17
Elliott, Wells, 118
Emancipation Day, 33, 128
Emigration, 5; to West Indies, 2; South to North, in U.S.A., 30; West Indies to U.S.A., 34, 38, 97; Garvey against, 41-42; Garveyites to Liberia, 90, 93; from West Indies, 5-8, 15, 69; to Costa Rica, 16; to England, 17, 71; to Lesotho, 26; to Panama, 38, 81; to Cuba, 69-71; to Dominican Republic, 74-75; to Latin America, 162; to South Africa, 87; to Liberia, 7
England, 3, 17, 40, 60, 81, 143; early history of Blacks in, 17-18; Garvey's early years in, 17-22; race riots, 1919, 71; UNIA in, 99; British hostility to UNIA, 101; Garvey's 1928 visit, 124-

26; plaque at Garvey's office, 157; Garvey's last years in, 141-47
Ethiopia, 28-29, 52, 53, 64, 77, 93, 122, 123, 142-44; and Rastafarians, 138-40
Ethiopian churches, 87-88
Europe, 2, 123; Garvey's 1928 visit, 124-26
Eyre, Edward John, 13, 14

Fanon, Frantz, 159
Ferris, William H., 21
Firestone Rubber Tire Company, 90
Fletcher, Sir Murchison, 72
Ford, Arnold J., 93, 139
Fortune, T. Thomas, 51-52, 86
France, 19, 99, 125
Frederick Douglass, S.S., 56, 58

Gambia, The, 7, 92
Gandhi, Mahatma, 64, 65
Garcia, Elie, 80, 89
Garvey, Amy Ashwood (wife No. 1), 30, 31, 88; marries Garvey, 66; divorce, 67
Garvey, Amy Jacques (wife No. 2), 16, 81, 126, 143, 152, 153, 155, 158; editor and writer, 67; *Philosophy and Opinions of Marcus Garvey,* 67, 158; marries Garvey, 67; *Garvey and Garveyism,* 153-54, 158;

awarded Musgrave Gold Medal, 156

Garvey, Indiana (sister), 8, 17, 30, 68

Garvey, Julius (son), 136

Garvey, Marcus, birth, 1; on coloureds, 4; fond of Blyden, 7; childhood and youth, 8-10; early years in Kingston, 10-14; and public speaking, 12, 13, 34; on Jamaica Rebellion, 13-14; in National Club, 14; to Costa Rica, 15; early travels in Central and South America, 15-17; publishes *La Prensa* and *La Nación*, 16; early travels in England and Europe, 17-22; publishes in *Africa Times and Orient Review*, 20-22; in Trinidad (1914), 27; founds UNIA, 27-37; on colour prejudice in Jamaica, 35; arrives in New York, 38; at Big Bethel AME Church, 40; speaks in England, 40; ideology, 48-54; on Black History, 52; elected provisional president of Africa, 61; and Third World solidarity, 64-65; marries Amy Ashwood, 66; at League of Nations, 66; escapes assassination, 66, 101-102; divorces Amy Ashwood, 67; marries Amy Jacques, 67; tours Cuba, 1921, 70; refused entry into Cuba, 71; Capt. Cipriani helps to enter Trinidad, 72-73; in Trinidad, 1937, 72-73; in-transit in Barbados, 1928, 76; in Barbados, 1937, 76; visits Belize, 1921 and 1930, 77, 78; tours Leeward and Windward Islands, 1937, 80; in Grenada, 1937, 80; refused entry into Bermuda, 1928, 81, 126; visits Costa Rica, 1921, 83; proposed African tour, 1923, 87; king of Swaziland on, 88; and Harry Thuku, 93; wants to relocate to Liberia, 100; Central American and Caribbean tour, 1921, 102; and courts, 104; mail fraud trial, imprisonment and deportation, 110-114; farewell speech at New Orleans, 114; stops in U.S.A., 1937, 114; in U.S. Canal Zone, 1927, 115-17; triumphant return to Jamaica, 1927, 116-24; in Jamaica, 1927-35, 115-40; on his work in the U.S.A., 123; European tour, 1928, 124-26; barred from English hotels, 124-25; as workers' representative, 126-27; fined for contempt of court, 129;

jailed in Jamaica, 132; on KSAC Council, 132–133, 135–136; loses legislative council election, 134–135; seditious libel case, 135; forms Jamaica Workers and Labourers Association, 136; farewell to Jamaica, 137, 141; and Rastafarians, 138–140; and Haile Selassie I, 139, 143-44; School of African Philosophy, 142; attacks Mussolini, 143; Bring Back Garvey campaign, 144–45; West Indian tour, 1937, 145–46; his arrival rumoured in Trinidad and Jamaica, 146; death, 147; underground hero, 148–52; international acclaim, 152-60; KSAC erects bust of, 152; his remains returned to Jamaica, 154; National Hero, 155; honoured by the African Studies Association of the West Indies, United Nations Special Committee Against Apartheid and the Organization of American States, 158–59; efforts to overturn his 1923 conviction, 159
Garvey, Marcus (father), 8, 9
Garvey, Marcus, Jr. (son), 136, 158

Garvey, Sarah (mother), 8, 9, 11
Garvey and Garveyism (Garvey), 153–54, 158
Garvey Day, 151
Garvey Release Week, 113
Garvey's Voice, 154
Garvey's Watchman, 13
General Goethals, S.S., 112
Germany, 19, 65, 125
Ghana, 55, 92, 94, 153
Gleaner. See *Daily Gleaner*
Globe Theatre, 73
Gold Coast. See Ghana
Gold Coast Leader, 92
Gordon, George William, 13, 14
Grant, St. William, 146
Greece (Ancient), 122–23, 138
Grenada, 27, 56, 59, 79, 80, 145
Guatemala, 6, 16, 37, 78, 83
Guinea, 7, 155
Guinea-Bissau, 95
Gumbs, J.G., 87
Guyana, 54, 57, 143, 145; immigration to, 5; Garvey's visit to, 1937, 74; UNIA in, 74

Haddon-Smith, Sir G.B., 79
Haiti, 14, 30, 70, 77, 80, 82, 89, 159; Dr. J. Robert Love in, 12
Harlem, 38–39, 42–47, 48, 56, 61, 67, 77, 92, 94, 123,

136, 152, 153; Negro Factories Corporation in, 54; Communists vs Garveyites in, 104; demonstration for Garvey's release, 113
Harlem Hospital, 66
Harrison, Hubert H., 43
Harvard University, 21
Hayford, J.E. Casely, 92
Haynes, Samuel A., 59, 77, 78
Ho Chi Minh, 64, 65
Holstein, Casper, 76
Holy Trinity Cathedral, 154
Honduras, 6, 37, 83, 150
Houénou, Kojo Tovalou, 94
House of Commons, 19
Human Rights Year, 155
Hungary, 19
Hutson, Governor Eyre, 78
Hyde Park, 19, 45, 141, 147, 151

India, 2, 64
Indo-China, 2
Industrial and Commercial Workers Union (ICU), 87, 104
Institute of Jamaica, 156
Integrationists, 106-09
International African Friends of Abyssinia, 143
International African Service Bureau, 141
International Conventions of the Negro Peoples of the World, 64, 102, 103; 1920, 59-64, 81, 89; 1922, 92; 1924, 94; 1929, 126-30, 148; 1934, 137, 139, 146; 1938, 145
International Peasants' Council, 113
International Seminar on Marcus Garvey, 158
Irish Easter uprising, 49
Italian-Ethiopian War. *See* Italo-Ethiopian War
Italo-Ethiopian War, 140, 142-44
Italy, 19, 28-29, 58-59

Jackson, D. Hamilton, 76
Jamaica, 1, 4, 14, 15, 18, 19, 27, 31, 32, 56, 57, 59, 66, 81, 82, 112, 143, 145; illiteracy in, 2; Jamaicans in Panama, 6; first Black legislative council member, 12; colour in, 35; UNIA conventions in, 64; emigration to Cuba from, 70; UNIA in, 73-74; maroons to Canada, 98; Garvey's return to, 1927, 116-24; Garvey in, 1927-35, 115-40
Jamaica Advocate, 12
Jamaican Secret Society of Coloured Men, 127
Jamaica Rebellion, 13, 134
James, C.L.R., 143
James Hon. Charles L., 142

Japan, 2
Java, 2
Johnson, Gabriel, 61, 89
Johnson, Jack, 86, 88

Kenawha (ship), 57
Kenya, 93, 125
Kenyatta, Johnstone. *See* Jomo
    Kenyatta
Kenyatta, Jomo, 93, 125
Kilroe, Edwin P., 101-02
Kimbangu, Simon, 94
King, Coretta Scott, 155
King, Martin Luther, Jr., 155
Kingston and St. Andrew
    Corporation (KSAC) Coun-
    cil, 113, 132, 152
Kipling, Rudyard, 51
Ku Klux Klan, 127

Lafayette Hall, 43
La Nación, 16
La Prensa, 16
League of Nations, 65-66, 80,
    125
Lenin, V. I., 65, 103
Lennon, Charles, 112
Lesotho, 26-27; UNIA in, 88
Liberia, 7, 28, 29, 53, 57, 60,
    61, 80, 95, 100, 101, 138,
    163; Barbadian immigra-
    tion to, 7; UNIA in, 88-90
Liberty Hall, 102; Harlem, 48,
    61, 66, 96; Belize, 77;
    Kingston, 113, 117, 118,
    120, 129, 143

Liberty League of Negro
    Americans, 43
Liga Africana, 95
Lindsay, John V., 157
London University, 3
L'Ouverture, Toussaint, 14,
    16, 61, 77
Love, Dr. J. Robert, 12

Mack, Judge Julian, 112
Madison Square Garden, 60,
    107
Malawi, 93, 94
Mandingoes, 7
Manning, Sir William H., 34
Mansfield, Lord, 18
Maraval, S.S., 56
Marcus Garvey Gardens, 157
Marcus Garvey Must Go!!!,
    109
Marcus Garvey Park Village,
    157
Marcus Garvey peace award,
    155
Marcus Garvey Scholarship for
    Boys, 155
Marcus Garvey Sundays, 113
Marke, George O., 92, 130,
    132
Marryshow, T.A., 79
Martí, José, 159
Martinique, 159
McGuire, Rev. George Alex-
    ander, 52, 78, 93
Menelik II, Emperor, 28
Menocal, President, 70

Mexico, 78, 83; West Indian
    emigration to, 6
Montserrat, 145
Morant Bay Rebellion. *See*
    Jamaica Rebellion
Morter, Isaiah Emanuel, 78
Moses, 77, 88, 117
Mozambique, 95
Muhammad, Elijah, 150
Mukasa, Reuben Spartas, 93
Mulzac, Hugh, 57
Muslims, 52
Mussolini, Benito, 142–44

Namibia, 88
National Association for the
    Advancement of Coloured
    People (NAACP), 106, 109
National Club, 14, 113
National Congress of British
    West Africa, 92
National Negro Voice, 151,
    152
Nation of Islam, 150
Negro Factories Corporation,
    54, 96, 104, 163
Negro World, 54–55, 59, 67,
    72, 74, 79, 88, 90, 96, 109,
    123, 137, 142, 162, 163;
    banned in various coun-
    tries, 54–55; and Indian
    struggle, 65; banned in Be-
    lize, 78, 101; and in St.
    Vincent, 79; banned in Ber-
    muda, 81; and in Costa
    Rica, 83; banned in French

Africa, 94; and in British
    West Africa, 92; banned in
    Kenya, 93; and in Malawi
    and Zambia, 94
Nembhard, Len S., 151
Nevis, 79, 145
New Jamaican, 137
Nicaragua, 6, 16, 37, 83
Nigeria, 20, 56, 69, 153; UNIA
    in, 90–92
Nkrumah, Kwame, 92, 153
Northern Rhodesia. *See* Zam-
    bia
Nyasaland. *See* Malawi

Organization of American
    States, 159
Oxford University, 3, 92

Padmore, George, 141, 159
Pan-African Conference, 8
Pan-Africanism, 12
Panama, 5, 6, 7, 16, 37, 38,
    56, 57, 60, 66, 71, 74, 80,
    83, 101, 112, 114, 115,
    150; West Indian emigra-
    tion to, 5, 7; UNIA in, 81–
    82
Panama Canal, 5–7, 82, 105
Paris Peace Conference, 65,
    80
Peart, Alfred, 30
Peart, Ruth, 118
People's Cooperative Bank, 74
People's Political Party, 130–36
Peru, 16

Philosophy and Opinions of Marcus Garvey (Garvey), 67, 92, 158
Phyllis Wheatley, S.S., 57
Port-of-Spain City Council, 72
Portugal, 2, 95
Printers' Union, 11
Puerto Rico, 81

Queen of Sheba, 77
Queens Royal College, 3

Rastafarians, 93, 138–40, 150
Red, black and green, 157, 160
Reggae music, 159
Republican Party, 47
Richards, Alfred, 72
Rio Pongo, 7
Royal Albert Hall, 125
Russia, 103
Russian Revolution, 49

Santa Marta, S.S., 117
Saramacca, S.S., 114, 115
Scarlett, Z. Monroe, 151, 152
School of African Philosophy, 142, 145
Scott, Emmett J., 41
Selassie I, Emperor Haile, 138–39, 142–44; awarded Black Star, 153
Selections from the Poetic Meditations of Marcus Garvey (Garvey), 113
Sen, Sun Yat, 64
Senegal, 94

Seymour, G. Seymour, 134
Shadyside, S.S., 56
Sierra Leone, 18, 92, 94
Simpson, H.A.L., 113, 121
Singleton, Rev. R.H., 40
Slavery, 1, 17, 18, 28, 29, 50, 86, 89, 128, 163
Smith, S.U., 148
Socialist Party, 47
Socrates, 116
Solanke, Ladipo, 125
Somerset, James, 18
South Africa, 8, 27, 60, 64, 69, 97, 101, 105, 106, 113, 141, 159; UNIA in, 87–88; Garveyites vs Communists in, 104
Southern Rhodesia. *See* Zimbabwe
South West Africa. *See* Namibia
Spain, 19
Speakers' Corner. *See* Hyde Park
St. Catherine District Prison, 132
St. Croix, 76–77
St. Croix Labour Union, 76
St. Eustatius, 80
St. George's Hall, 124
St. Kitts, 57, 79, 105, 145
St. Lucia, 143, 145, 150; UNIA in, 79
St. Mark's Roman Catholic Church Hall, 39
St. Mary's College, 2
St. Thomas, 7, 76–77

St. Vincent, 57, 79, 143, 145
Sudan, 20, 52
Suriname, 80
Swaziland, 88
Switzerland, 80, 125-26
Syria, 134

Tafari, Ras. *See* Haile Selassie I
Thaele, James, 87
Third World, 64-65
Thuku, Harry, 93
Tobitt, Rev. Richard Hilton, 76, 80, 81
Touré, Sékou, 155
Tragedy of White Injustice, The (Garvey), 113
Trials and Triumphs of Marcus Garvey (Nembhard), 151
Trinidad and Tobago, 3, 7, 8, 16, 54, 56, 57, 59, 60, 64, 70, 141, 143, 150, 151, 159; immigration to, 5; Garvey in, 1914, 27; 1919 unrest in, 59; UNIA in, 71-73, 79; Rev. Tobitt refused entry, 80; Garvey's 1937 visit, 145-46
Trinidad Workingmen's Association, 27, 59, 71, 72
Trotsky, Leon, 103
Tudor, James A., 75, 76
Tuskegee Institute, 25, 36, 41
Tyler, George, 66, 101-02

Uganda, 93, 155
UNIA. *See* Universal Negro Improvement Association

Union Island, 57
United Fruit Company, 15, 16, 82, 117, 126; gives Garvey VIP treatment, 83
United Nations, 65, 157
United Nations Special Committee Against Apartheid, 159
United States, 12; West Indian immigration to, 6, 7, 34, 38; official hostility towards Garvey, 101-02; Garvey's account of his work in, 123
United States Canal Zone, 81, 82, 115
Universal African Legions, 60, 112
Universal African Nationalist Movement, 150
Universal Ethiopian Anthem, 64, 120, 138, 139
Universal Negro Improvement and Conservation Association and African Communities (Imperial) League. *See* Universal Negro Improvement Association
Universal Negro Improvement Association (UNIA), 141; in Trinidad and Tobago, 27, 71; birth of, 27-37; aims and objects, 31-32; in Harlem, 46, 76, 77, 105; incorporated in New York, 48; in Cuba, 69-71; in Dominican Republic, 75; in

Belize, 77-78; in Antigua, 78; "Tiger" division, Brooklyn, 146; in Jamaica, 118, 123, 129-30, 139, 143, 148, 159; in Dominica, 78; in Nevis, 79; in St. Kitts, 79; in St. Lucia, 79; in St. Vincent, 79; in Grenada, 79-80; in Suriname, 80; in Aruba, 80; in Haiti, 80; in San Francisco, 80; in Bermuda, 81; in Puerto Rico, 81; in Panama, 81-82; in Costa Rica, 82-83; in South Africa, 87; in Lesotho, 88; in Namibia, 88; in Liberia, 88-90; in Nigeria, 90-92; in Ghana, 92; in Sierra Leone, 92; in Afro-America, 96-98, 154; in England, 99; in Wales, 99; as provisional African nation, 100; begins to fragment, 136-37; and Rastafarians, 139; in 1980s, 142; Jamaica conference, 1978, 159; UNIA dramatic company, 127; UNIA band, 128

Universal Negro Improvement Association and African Communities League (August 1929) of the World, 129

Universal Negro Improvement Association Choir, 127

Universal Negro Improvement Association, Inc., 129

Universal Negro Improvement Association Juveniles, 61

Universal Jazz Hounds, 127

University of the West Indies, 158

Up From Slavery (Washington), 25, 26

Van Winkle, Rip, 42

Venezuela, 6, 83

Victoria, Queen, 8

Victoria Market Pier, 11, 154

Vietnam, 64, 65

Virgin Islands Federation of Labour, 76-77

Von Ketelhodt, Baron, 14

Wales, 99

Walker, Johnnie, 148

Ward Theatre, 121, 123

Washington, Booker T., 20, 36-37; *Up From Slavery*, 25

Watchman, The, 13

West African Students' Union (WASU), 125

West Indian Federation, 21, 131

West India Royal Commission, 146

West Indian, The, 79

West Indians, race and colour, 4; emigration from West Indies, 5-8, 15, 69; emigration to Costa Rica, 16; to England, 17, 71; to Lesotho, 26; to U.S.A.,

34, 38, 97; to Panama, 38, 81; Garvey opposes West Indian emigration, 41–42; emigration to Cuba, 69–71; to Dominican Republic, 74–75; to Latin America, 162; to South Africa, 87; to Liberia, 7
Weston, George, 78
Westwood Training College for Women, 36
Wheatley, Phillis, 57
Williams, Francis, 3
Williams, Henry Sylvester, 8, 159
Wint, Dunbar Theophilus, 134
Woman question, 32, 33, 41

Woodford Square, 73
Workers and Labourers Association, 136
World War I, 34, 49, 58, 65, 80, 161–62
World War II, 57

X, Malcolm, 150

Yale University, 21
Yarmouth, S. S., 55
Yorubas (in Trinidad), 143

Zaire, 8, 29, 94
Zambia, 93
Zampty, J. Charles, 16
Zimbabwe, 55, 94
Zipporah, 77